DATE DUE

*M*odern *M*iddle *E*ast *N*ati*⊕*ns
AND THEIR STRATEGIC PLACE IN THE WORLD

FACTS & FIGURES
ABOUT THE MIDDLE EAST

Modern Middle East Nations
AND THEIR STRATEGIC PLACE IN THE WORLD

FACTS & FIGURES
ABOUT THE MIDDLE EAST

LISA McCOY

MASON CREST PUBLISHERS
PHILADELPHIA

Produced by OTTN Publishing, Stockton, New Jersey

Mason Crest Publishers
370 Reed Road
Broomall, PA 19008
www.masoncrest.com

3 5 7 9 8 6 4 2

Library of Congress Cataloging-in-Publication Data

Applied for

ISBN: 1-59084-528-5

Modern Middle East Nations
AND THEIR STRATEGIC PLACE IN THE WORLD

TABLE OF CONTENTS

Modern Middle East Nations

AND THEIR STRATEGIC PLACE IN THE WORLD

Dr. Harvey Sicherman, president and director of the Foreign Policy Research Institute, is the author of such books as *America the Vulnerable: Our Military Problems and How to Fix Them* (2002) and *Palestinian Autonomy, Self-Government and Peace* (1993).

Introduction

by Dr. Harvey Sicherman

Situated as it is between Africa, Europe, and the Far East, the Middle East has played a unique role in world history. Often described as the birthplace of religions (notably Judaism, Christianity, and Islam) and the cradle of civilizations (Egypt, Mesopotamia, Persia), this region and its peoples have given humanity some of its most precious possessions. At the same time, the Middle East has had more than its share of conflicts. The area is strewn with the ruins of fortifications and the cemeteries of combatants, not to speak of modern arsenals for war.

Today, more than ever, Americans are aware that events in the Middle East can affect our security and prosperity. The United States has a considerable military, political, and economic presence throughout much of the region. Developments there regularly find their way onto the front pages of our newspapers and the screens of our television sets.

Still, it is fair to say that most Middle Eastern countries remain a mystery, their cultures and religions barely known, their peoples and politics confusing and strange. The purpose of this book series is to change that, to educate the reader in the basic facts about the 23 states and many peoples that make up the region. (For our purpose, the Middle East also includes the North African states linked by ethnicity, language, and religion to the Arabs, as well as Somalia and Mauritania, which are African but share the Muslim religion and are members of the Arab League.) A notable feature of the series is the integration of geography, demography, and history; economics and politics; culture and religion. The careful student will learn much that he or she needs to know about ever so important lands.

A few general observations are in order as an introduction to the subject matter.

The first has to do with history and politics. The modern Middle East is full of ancient sites and peoples who trace their lineage and literature to antiquity. Many commentators also attribute the Middle East's political conflicts to grievances and rivalries from the distant past. While history is often invoked, the truth is that the modern Middle East political system dates only from the 1920s and was largely created by the British and the French, the victors of World War I. Such states as Algeria, Iraq, Israel, Jordan, Kuwait, Saudi Arabia, Syria, Turkey, and the United Arab Emirates did not exist before 1914—they became independent between 1920 and 1971. Others, such as Egypt and Iran, were dominated by outside powers until well after World War II. Before 1914, most of the region's states were either controlled by the Turkish-run Ottoman Empire or owed allegiance to the Ottoman sultan. (The sultan was also the caliph or highest religious authority in Islam, in the line of the prophet Muhammad's successors, according to the beliefs of the majority of Muslims known as the *Sunni*.) It was this imperial Muslim system that was ended by the largely British military victory over the Ottomans in World War I. Few of the leaders who emerged in the wake of this event were happy with the territories they were assigned or the borders, which were often drawn by Europeans. Yet, the system has endured despite many efforts to change it.

The second observation has to do with economics, demography, and natural resources. The Middle Eastern peoples live in a region of often dramatic geographical contrasts: vast parched deserts and high mountains, some with year-round snow; stone-hard volcanic rifts and lush semi-tropical valleys; extremely dry and extremely wet conditions, sometimes separated by only a few miles; large permanent rivers and wadis, riverbeds dry as a bone until winter rains send torrents of flood from the mountains to the sea. In ancient times, a very skilled agriculture made the Middle East the breadbasket of the Roman Empire, and its trade carried luxury fabrics, foods, and spices both East and West.

Most recently, however, the Middle East has become more known for a single commodity—oil, which is unevenly distributed and largely concentrated in the Persian Gulf and Arabian Peninsula (although large pockets are also to be found in Algeria, Libya, and other sites). There are also new, potentially lucrative offshore gas fields in the Eastern Mediterranean.

This uneven distribution of wealth has been compounded by demographics. Birth rates are very high, but the countries with the most oil are often lightly populated. Over the last decade, Middle East populations under the age of 20 have grown enormously. How will these young people be educated? Where will they work? The failure of most governments in the region to give their people skills and jobs (with notable exceptions such as Israel) has also contributed to large out-migrations. Many have gone to Europe; many others work in other Middle Eastern countries, supporting their families from afar.

Another unsettling situation is the heavy pressure both people and industry have put on vital resources. Chronic water shortages plague the region. Air quality, public sanitation, and health services in the big cities are also seriously overburdened. There are solutions to these problems, but they require a cooperative approach that is sorely lacking.

A third important observation is the role of religion in the Middle East. Americans, who take separation of church and state for granted, should know that most countries in the region either proclaim their countries to be Muslim or allow a very large role for that religion in public life. Among those with predominantly Muslim populations, Turkey alone describes itself as secular and prohibits avowedly religious parties in the political system. Lebanon was a Christian-dominated state, and Israel continues to be a Jewish state. While both strongly emphasize secular politics, religion plays an enormous role in culture, daily life, and legislation. It is also important to recall that Islamic law (*Sharia*) permits people to practice Judaism and Christianity in Muslim states but only as *Dhimmi*, protected but very second-class citizens.

Fourth, the American student of the modern Middle East will be impressed by the varieties of one-man, centralized rule, very unlike the workings of Western democracies. There are monarchies, some with traditional methods of consultation for tribal elders and even ordinary citizens, in Saudi Arabia and many Gulf States; kings with limited but still important parliaments (such as in Jordan and

Morocco); and military and civilian dictatorships, some (such as Syria) even operating on the hereditary principle (Hafez al Assad's son Bashar succeeded him). Turkey is a practicing democracy, although a special role is given to the military that limits what any government can do. Israel operates the freest democracy, albeit constricted by emergency regulations (such as military censorship) due to the Arab-Israeli conflict.

In conclusion, the MODERN MIDDLE EAST NATIONS series will engage imagination and interest simply because it covers an area of such great importance to the United States. Americans may be relative latecomers to the affairs of this region, but our involvement there will endure. We at the Foreign Policy Research Institute hope that these books will kindle a lifelong interest in the fascinating and significant Middle East.

The Middle East is the birthplace of three of the world's great monotheistic religions—Judaism, Christianity, and Islam. Followers of all three faiths consider Jerusalem a holy city. The Dome of the Rock, a shrine for Muslim pilgrims built in Jerusalem during the late seventh century A.D., is built on the site of earlier Jewish temples.

The Middle East Today

T he Middle East is a vast region, generally considered to encompass 23 countries: Jordan, Egypt, Syria, Libya, Kuwait, Lebanon, Morocco, Iraq, Algeria, Somalia, Oman, Tunisia, Sudan, Saudi Arabia, United Arab Emirates, Qatar, Bahrain, Yemen, Turkey, Djibouti, Mauritania, Israel, and Iran. Westerners created the term "Middle East," and at first the peoples of this region did not use this term to designate where they lived. But in modern times many Middle Eastern peoples have adopted it, particularly those who speak English as a second or third language. (The term "Near East," coined by British scholars and statesmen, refers to the same general area. This phrase is still in use in some places. For example, the U.S. Department of State refers to the office that is concerned with this section of the world as the Bureau of Near Eastern Affairs.)

Definitions of what constitutes the Middle East or the

Near East differ. Some experts do not consider Mauritania, Somalia, and Djibouti to be Middle Eastern countries because many of the people in these countries do not speak Arabic, Turkish, Persian, or Hebrew as their native language. They are included here because they are members of the Arab League. Some definitions also include the country of Afghanistan, which is not included in this book. Geographical definitions also vary from culture to culture. Russian and Chinese scholars, for example, divide up regions of the world differently than American and British scholars do.

Within the region of the Middle East, as established above, there are several sub-regions. One is North Africa, which Arabs call the Maghreb. The area directly to the south, which most people do not include in the Middle East but which does contain Mauritania, is called the Sahel. Most Arabs refer to the Asian parts of the Middle East region as the Mashrakh. The eastern Mediterranean area is sometimes referred to by the old French term "the Levant." The term "Gulf states" identifies the countries along the coasts of the Persian Gulf, although the Arab countries prefer to call that body of water the Arabian Gulf or Arabian Sea.

Before going further, a few other terms should be properly defined. Among many people who are not specialists in politics and history, the terms "nation," "country," and "state" are often used interchangeably. This usage is incorrect, however. A nation is a group of people who consider themselves to have important characteristics in common. In modern terms, a nation is a group of people who believe themselves to be entitled—or are believed by others to be entitled—to exist as an independent country. A country is the physical space in which the nation lives. The state is the governmental apparatus that rules the nation in the country. The term "nation-state" is a term that signifies a peaceful relationship between the nation being ruled and the members of the small group that governs it. Most members of the United Nations today are too

These ancient statues on Mount Nemrut, in present-day Turkey, are all that remains of a royal burial ground from an ancient empire that was settled in the region more than 2,000 years ago. The carvings show both Hellenistic and Persian influences.

heterogeneous to really be nation-states; typically, a dominant group within these countries rules other groups.

These are important distinctions when we talk about the Middle East, because while Westerners generally refer to the countries of this region as "nations," the term is not entirely accurate. The concept of a nation was originally a Western idea, and it is not yet completely embraced in much of the Middle East. Many people who live in heterogeneous countries, like Lebanon or Iraq, have a tenuous association with what we may call a Lebanese nation or an Iraqi nation. Instead, they associate and identify themselves either with religious groups and ethnic groups, or families and clans. Another important distinction to make about the Middle East is that many of the region's countries have only recently won their independence. The people of the newer countries are still in the early stages of shaping their identity, which is another reason nationhood is less of a driving force here than it is in North America, Europe, and most of Asia. It is important to keep this in mind when studying the Middle East.

When one thinks of the Middle East, some images may easily come to mind: oil fields, deserts with sand dunes, camels, **Bedouins** in tents, oases with palm trees. All of these things can be found in the Middle East, but a full picture of the region has much more than the all-familiar sights. Deserts do take up major portions of lands in the Middle East, but few of these deserts consist of sand dunes and nothing else. There are deserts that experience heavy rainfalls—and even snow. Nevertheless, the lack of water is a critical issue in much of the region, particularly as populations grow to levels heretofore unknown in the history of the Middle East.

Oil—another critical issue—is a primary commodity for many countries in the Middle East and has played a significant role in the region's modern history, especially the Gulf states. But there are countries that do not rely on oil as a source of revenue at all. The Middle Eastern countries with reserves of oil usually have a higher standard of living than those that don't have reserves. However, Israel, which has no oil at all, is one of the wealthiest countries in the region on a per capita basis. And there are Arab countries without oil reserves, such as Jordan, that have more diversified economies and better educational systems than the Arab countries with large oil reserves.

The history of the Middle East is a very long and complex one. This region is the cradle of human civilization and the site of the agricultural revolution. Many empires have formed within the

Middle East, and others that formed outside the region have conquered parts of the Middle East. Determining the region's original inhabitants is difficult for two reasons: First, the overarching influence of the empires did not let peoples stand isolated from those that conquered them. Second, with the Middle East situated at a crossroads between Africa and Asia, and Europe just across the Mediterranean Sea, groups of people were always moving and mixing with other groups. It is extremely difficult to pinpoint a time when this ethnic mixing did not take place. Groups eventually formed identities, though from ancient times to the present, group names and languages have changed often.

Before modern times, there were only two social groups, and their identities were based more on their settlement patterns than specific cultural traits. There were Bedouin, or nomads, and there were *hadhari*, or sedentary dwellers, who usually lived along river banks or at the base of hills where rain fell. There were two types of nomads: what anthropologists call "horizontal" nomads, those who went from place to place looking for pasture and water; and "vertical" nomads, those who moved between high and low elevations depending on the season.

In the 21st century, there are very few nomads left in the Middle East. The people who live in the region today include Arabs, Iranians (Persians), Turks, and Jews, and, on the fringes of the region, Somalis, Tuareg, Berbers, Kurds, Baluchis, Pashtuns, Nubians, and some others. But there also is Armenian, Greek, Roman, Portuguese, Spanish, French, Dinka, Mongol, and other "blood" in the peoples of the Middle East.

The main binding force of the Middle East, and the region's defining characteristic today, is Islamic culture. Islam is a religion, considered the third of the Abrahamic faiths (Judaism and Christianity are the other two), and its followers are called Muslims. While not all peoples in the Middle East are Muslims, and while

Colorful and intricate tile patterns like this are common in the countries of the Middle East. Because Islam does not allow living things such as people, animals, or plants to be depicted in art, artists often decorate buildings with detailed geometric patterns.

many Muslims live outside the Middle East in countries such as Indonesia, Pakistan, Bangladesh, and Afghanistan, Islamic culture pervades the history, the art, the literature, and the consciousness of the region.

Religion is an extremely important component to life in the Middle East, and while Islam is the dominant religion, Christianity and Judaism also have a definite presence. Several prominent conflicts in modern Middle Eastern history have been influenced by religion, like the 1979 Iranian Revolution and the ongoing Arab-Israeli conflict, but these are not primarily religious wars and should not be labeled as such. Nonetheless, religion is inextricably tied to politics in the Middle East, and a solid understanding of Islam helps students better understand the culture and politics of the region as a whole.

The Middle East is an important area of the world for political, cultural, economic and security-related reasons, but it is also often misunderstood by many Westerners. Unfortunately, it is only possible to briefly cover each of the countries here. As an overview, however, this book can give the reader a better understanding of the Middle East in the areas of geography, history, religion, people, and major communities. For more detailed information on any particular country, readers should consult the individual books in the MODERN MIDDLE EAST NATIONS series.

A woman leads a camel through the desert, which covers large areas of the Middle East. For thousands of years people living in the harsh deserts of the Arabian Peninsula and North Africa depended on camels for transportation, as well as for meat, milk, hides, and wool.

The Land

T he Middle East is a vast and diverse region, both politically and geographically. While most people in North America and Europe might hear "the Middle East" and think of the empty expanse of desert depicted in books and films, reality presents a different picture. People who visit the Middle East for the first time are often surprised that it doesn't always match their expectations.

Of course, the desert, comprising a large part of the Middle East's geography, is not a natural feature that can be ignored. But the region also includes coral reefs of the Red Sea, which draw large numbers of scuba divers; permanent snowfields and *cirque* glaciers on the slopes of Mount Ararat in eastern Turkey and Mount Damavand in Iran; salt-crusted flats and evaporation pans in central Iran and in the countries of North Africa, and the coastal marshes and wetlands of the Nile Delta. Given the diversity of the Middle East's geography,

An oasis at Tafraout, Morocco. An oasis is a fertile area in a desert where plants grow and water is available.

therefore, the best way to present it is to focus on geographical features individually.

As discussed in the first chapter, the Middle East has an ever-changing identity, which can confuse a discussion of a topic such as geography. Some Middle Eastern countries have undefined boundaries, often because those boundaries are currently the subject of dispute among neighboring countries. Throughout the region's history, nations have been swallowed up or have become fragmented, expanding or shrinking a country's land. And sometimes the inhabitants of countries have traditional perceptions of their boundaries that do not quite agree with the understanding of others. For example, Egyptians still call their country Misr, which originally referred only to the Nile Delta and its narrow valley, not to the other territory contained within Egypt's present boundaries.

While the term "Middle East" is becoming more common, particularly in dialogues between Westerners and people of the region, people forget how recently the term was coined. As a place designation, the "Middle East" was first used in 1902 by British naval strategists in the Arabian Gulf. The term soon gained wider acceptance, as the British used it to refer to an area of strategic concern located between the remnants of the Ottoman Empire in the Near East, the Russian empire in Central Asia, and the much-prized British colony in India. As more time passed, the term "Middle East" became a universal term in military language, first among officers fighting in World War I, then by the international peace-keeping agencies that formed in the wake of the two world wars.

Today, it is largely understood that the Middle East encompasses countries that share a common history. These countries stretch in a long band from the North Atlantic Ocean to the Indian Ocean and the Arabian Sea and encompass parts of two continents, Africa and Asia.

ARIDITY AND WATER

An important component in the geography of the Middle East—perhaps the most important—is the presence or absence of water. This has decided for generations what crops, if any, could be farmed and when. The degree of **aridity** varies widely throughout the Middle East. The winter months bring rainfall to many areas, especially those at higher elevations in the north. Heavy snowfalls are not uncommon in these areas, and neither is heavy spring flooding when this snow melts. As one moves south, however, rainstorms occur less frequently and the amount of annual rainfall decreases. Some areas of the Arabian Peninsula may receive as little as 4 inches (10 cm) of rain a year.

In previous centuries, the various peoples of the Middle East often used groundwater from **aquifers**, along with a basin-irrigation system, to grow crops. These traditional water-management systems worked well, as is clear from the fact that they were in use well into the 19th century and were adapted to fit local conditions all over the Middle East, North Africa, and even Spain and the New World. These systems supported very large populations, though not as large as in the 20th century. As the population continues to grow in the Middle East, so does the demand for water, and newer and more efficient irrigation systems have displaced traditional systems in many areas. But new technologies have caused harm along with improving efficiency. For example, while the construction of the Aswan High Dam in Egypt enabled the regular irrigation of crops, it has also led to serious environmental side effects, such as soil **salinization**.

The availability and management of water still presents a challenge to the countries of the Middle East. This problem overlaps with disputes over boundaries in some cases. Studies show that roughly two-thirds of the water supply available to Arab countries has its source in non-Arab countries. Given this fact, it is hardly surprising that water rights and water allocation have been important issues in peace negotiations.

THE LAND: AN OVERVIEW

The total land area of the Middle East is 2.8 million square miles (7.3 million sq km). Much of the region consists of flat plains or plateaus. In general, the northern part of the Middle East is more mountainous and receives more rain, whereas in the south, the climate is more arid, there is less rainfall, and desert is the dominant feature of the landscape.

Temperatures also vary throughout the Middle East. For example, in Turkey, the average winter temperature is around 32°F (0°C) and the average summer temperature is around 73°F (23°C). By contrast, western Saudi Arabia has an average winter temperature of 75°F (24°C) and an average summer temperature of 89°F (31°C).

Mountains rise over a resort on the Mediterranean coast of southern Turkey.

For many of the countries of the Middle East, there are no major rivers or other navigable waterways. Some countries, like the island country of Bahrain, have no natural freshwater sources at all. The main exceptions are the Nile River, which supplies water to Egypt; the Tigris and Euphrates rivers, which supply water to Iraq, Syria, and Turkey; the Jordan River, which supplies water to Israel; the Yarmuk River, which supplies irrigation canals in Jordan, and the Orontes and Barada rivers in Syria. There are also several large rivers that flow from the Zagros Mountains through Iran and from the Taurus Mountains through Turkey.

Geography of the Middle East

Algeria

Total area: 919,590 square miles (2,381,740 sq km)
  land: 919,590 square miles (2,381,740 sq km)
  water: 0 square miles

Climate: arid to semiarid; mild, wet winters with hot, dry summers along coast; drier with cold winters and hot summers on high plateau; sirocco is a hot, dust/sand-laden wind especially common in summer

Terrain: mostly high plateau and desert; some mountains; narrow, discontinuous coastal plain

Elevation extremes:
  lowest point: Chott Melrhir, 131 feet (40 meters) below sea level
  highest point: Tahat, 9,852 feet (3,003 meters)

Bahrain

Total area: 257 square miles (665 sq km)
  land: 257 square miles (665 sq km)
  water: 0 square miles

Climate: arid; mild, pleasant winters; very hot, humid summers

Terrain: mostly low desert plain rising gently to low central escarpment

Elevation extremes:
  lowest point: Persian Gulf, 0 feet
  highest point: Jabal ad Dukhan, 400 feet (122 meters)

Djibouti

Total area: 8,880 square miles (23,000 sq km)
  land: 8872 square miles (22,980 sq km)
  water: 8 square miles (20 sq km)

Climate: desert; torrid, dry

Terrain: coastal plain and plateau separated by central mountains

Elevation extremes:
  lowest point: Lac Assal, 509 feet (155 meters) below sea level
  highest point: Moussa Ali, 6,654 feet (2,028 meters)

Egypt

Total area: 386,660 square miles (1,001,450 sq km)
  land: 384,343 square miles (995,450 sq km)
  water: 2,317 square miles (6,000 sq km)

Climate: desert; hot, dry summers with moderate winters

Terrain: vast desert plateau interrupted by Nile valley and delta

Elevation extremes:
  lowest point: Qattara depression, 436 feet (133 meters) below sea level
  highest point: Mount Catherine, 8,625 feet (2,629 meters)

Iran

Total area: 636,293 square miles (1,648,000 sq km)
  land: 631,660 square miles (1,636,000 sq km)
  water: 4,633 square miles (12,000 sq km)

Climate: mostly arid or semiarid, subtropical along Caspian coast

Terrain: rugged, mountainous rim; high, central basin with deserts, mountains; small, discontinuous plains along both coasts

Elevation extremes:
  lowest point: Caspian Sea, 92 feet (28 meters) below sea level
  highest point: Qolleh-ye Damavand, 18,605 feet (5,671 meters)

Iraq

Total area: 168,754 square miles (437,072 sq km)
  land: 166,858 square miles (432,162 sq km)
  water: 1,896 square miles (4,910 sq km)

Climate: mostly desert; mild to cool winters with dry, hot, cloudless summers; northern mountainous regions along Iranian and Turkish borders experience cold winters with occasionally heavy snows that melt in early spring, sometimes causing extensive flooding in central and southern Iraq

Terrain: mostly broad plains; reedy marshes

along Iranian border in south with large flooded areas; mountains along borders with Iran and Turkey

Elevation extremes:
  lowest point: Persian Gulf, 0 feet
  highest point: Haji Ibrahim, 11,811 feet (3,600 meters)

Israel

Total area: 8,019 square miles (20,770 sq km)
  land: 7,849 square miles (20,330 sq km)
  water: 170 square miles (440 sq km)

climate: temperate; hot and dry in southern and eastern desert areas

Terrain: Negev desert in the south; low coastal plain; central mountains; Jordan Rift Valley

Elevation extremes:
  lowest point: Dead Sea, 1,339 feet (408 meters) below sea level
  highest point: Har Meron, 3,963 feet (1,208 meters)

Jordan

Total area: 35,637 square miles (92,300 sq km)
  land: 35,510 square miles (91,971 sq km)
  water: 127 square miles (329 sq km)

Climate: mostly arid desert; rainy season in west (November to April)

Terrain: mostly desert plateau in east, highland area in west; Great Rift Valley separates East and West Banks of the Jordan River

Elevation extremes:
  lowest point: Dead Sea, 1,339 feet (408 meters) below sea level
  highest point: Jabal Ram, 5,689 feet (1,734 meters)

Kuwait

Total area: 6,880 square miles (17,820 sq km)
  land: 6,880 square miles (17,820 sq km)
  water: 0 square miles

Climate: dry desert; intensely hot summers; short, cool winters

Terrain: flat to slightly undulating desert plain

Elevation extremes:
  lowest point: Persian Gulf, 0 feet
  highest point: unnamed location, 1004 feet (306 meters)

Lebanon

Total area: 4,016 square miles (10,400 sq km)
  land: 3,950 square miles (10,230 sq km)
  water: 66 square miles (170 sq km)

Climate: Mediterranean; mild to cool, wet winters with hot, dry summers; Lebanon mountains experience heavy winter snows

Terrain: narrow coastal plain; El Beqaa (Bekaa Valley) separates Lebanon and Anti-Lebanon Mountains

Elevation extremes:
  lowest point: Mediterranean Sea, 0 feet
  highest point: Qurnat as Sawda', 10,131 feet (3,088 meters)

Libya

Total area: 679,358 square miles (1,759,540 sq km)
  land: 679,358 square miles (1,759,540 sq km)
  water: 0 square miles

Climate: Mediterranean along coast; dry, extreme desert interior

Terrain: mostly barren, flat to undulating plains, plateaus, depressions

Elevation extremes:
  lowest point: Sabkhat Ghuzayyil, 154 feet (47 meters) below sea level
  highest point: Bikku Bitti, 7,438 feet (2,267 meters)

Mauritania

Total area: 397,953 square miles (1,030,700 sq km)
  land: 397,837 square miles (1,030,400 sq km)
  water: 116 square miles (300 sq km)

Climate: desert; constantly hot, dry, dusty

Terrain: mostly barren, flat plains of the Sahara; some central hills

Elevation extremes:
  lowest point: Sebkha de Ndrhamcha, 10 feet (3 meters) below sea level
  highest point: Kediet Ijill, 2,986 feet (910 meters)

Morocco

Total area: 172,413 square miles (446,550 sq km)
  land: 172,316 square miles (446,300 sq km)

water: 97 square miles (250 sq km)

Climate: Mediterranean, becoming more extreme in the interior

Terrain: northern coast and interior are mountainous with large areas of bordering plateaus, intermontane valleys, and rich coastal plains

Elevation extremes:
  lowest point: Sebkha Tah, 180 feet (55 meters) below sea level
  highest point: Jebel Toubkal, 13,665 feet (4,165 meters)

Oman

Total area: 82,031 square miles (212,460 sq km)
  land: 82,031 square miles (212,460 sq km)
  water: 0 square miles

Climate: dry desert; hot, humid along coast; hot, dry interior; strong southwest summer monsoon (May to September) in far south

Terrain: central desert plain, rugged mountains in north and south

Elevation extremes:
  lowest point: Arabian Sea, 0 feet
  highest point: Jabal Shams, 9777 feet (2,980 meters)

Qatar

Total area: 4,416 square miles (11,437 sq km)
  land: 4,416 square miles (11,437 sq km)
  water: 0 square miles

Climate: arid; mild, pleasant winters; very hot, humid summers

Terrain: mostly flat and barren desert covered with loose sand and gravel

Elevation extremes:
  lowest point: Persian Gulf, 0 feet
  highest point: Qurayn Abu al Bawl, 338 feet (103 meters)

Saudi Arabia

Total area: 756,981 square miles (1,960,582 sq km)
  land: 756,981 square miles (1,960,582 sq km)
  water: 0 square miles

Climate: harsh, dry desert with great temperature extremes

Terrain: mostly uninhabited, sandy desert

Elevation extremes:
  lowest point: Persian Gulf, 0 feet
  highest point: Jabal Sawda', 10,279 feet (3,133 meters)

Somalia

Total area: 246,199 square miles (637,657 sq km)
  land: 242,215 square miles (627,337 sq km)
  water: 3,984 square miles (10,320 sq km)

Climate: principally desert; December to February—northeast monsoon, moderate temperatures in north and very hot in south; May to October—southwest monsoon, torrid in the north and hot in the south, irregular rainfall, hot and humid periods (tangambili) between monsoons

Terrain: mostly flat to undulating plateau rising to hills in north

Elevation extremes:
  lowest point: Indian Ocean, 0 feet
  highest point: Shimbiris, 7926 feet (2,416 meters)

Sudan

Total area: 967,493 square miles (2,505,810 sq km)
  land: 917,373 square miles (2,376,000 sq km)
  water: 50,120 square miles (129,810 sq km)

Climate: tropical in south; arid desert in north; rainy season (April to October)

Terrain: generally flat, featureless plain; mountains in east and west

Elevation extremes:
  lowest point: Red Sea, 0 feet
  highest point: Kinyeti, 10,456 feet (3,187 meters)

Syria

Total area: 71,498 square miles (185,180 sq km)
  land: 71,062 square miles (184,050 sq km)
  water: 436 square miles (1,130 sq km)

Climate: mostly desert; hot, dry, sunny summers (June to August) and mild, rainy winters (December to February) along coast; cold weather with snow or sleet periodically in Damascus

Terrain: primarily semiarid and desert plateau; narrow coastal plain; mountains in west

Elevation extremes:
 lowest point: unnamed location near Lake Tiberias, 656 feet (200 meters) below sea level
 highest point: Mount Hermon, 9,232 feet (2,814 meters)

Tunisia

Total area: 63,170 square miles (163,610 sq km)
 land: 59,985 square miles (155,360 sq km)
 water: 3,185 square miles (8,250 sq km)

Climate: temperate in north with mild, rainy winters and hot, dry summers; desert in south

Terrain: mountains in north; hot, dry central plain; semiarid south merges into the Sahara

Elevation extremes:
 lowest point: Shatt al Gharsah, 56 feet (17 meters) below sea level
 highest point: Jebel ech Chambi, 5,066 feet (1,544 meters)

Turkey

Total area: 301,382 square miles (780,580 sq km)
 land: 297,590 square miles (770,760 sq km)
 water: 3,792 square miles (9,820 sq km)

Climate: temperate; hot, dry summers with mild, wet winters; harsher in interior

Terrain: mostly mountains; narrow coastal plain; high central plateau (Anatolia)

Elevation extremes:
 lowest point: Mediterranean Sea, 0 feet
 highest point: Mount Ararat, 16,949 feet (5,166 meters)

United Arab Emirates

Total area: 32,000 square miles (82,880 sq km)
 land: 32,000 square miles (82,880 sq km)
 water: 0 square miles

Climate: desert; cooler in eastern mountains

Terrain: flat, barren coastal plain merging into rolling sand dunes of vast desert wasteland; mountains in east

Elevation extremes:
 lowest point: Persian Gulf, 0 feet
 highest point: Jabal Yibir, 5,010 feet (1,527 meters)

Yemen

Total area: 203,849 square miles (527,970 sq km)
 land: 203,849 square miles (527,970 sq km)
 water: 0 square miles

Climate: mostly desert; hot and humid along west coast; temperate in western mountains affected by seasonal monsoon; extraordinarily hot, dry, harsh desert in east

Terrain: narrow coastal plain backed by flat-topped hills and rugged mountains; dissected upland desert plains in center slope into the desert interior of the Arabian Peninsula

Elevation extremes:
 lowest point: Arabian Sea, 0 feet
 highest point: Jabal an Nabi Shu'ayb, 12,336 feet (3,760 meters)

Source: Adapted from CIA World Factbook, 2002.

U.S. soldiers pose with flag-waving Kuwaitis and Saudis at the end of the 1991 Persian Gulf War. After Iraq invaded its tiny neighbor Kuwait in the summer of 1990, the United States marshaled an international coalition of nations to force the Iraqi army to withdraw.

History

A significant feature of Middle Eastern history is the pattern of invasion and conquest. Persia, Greece, Rome, the Arabs, the Seljuk Turks, the Mongols, the Ottomans, the French, and the British have all had empires that claimed some or a large portion of the Middle East.

The introduction of Hellenistic culture, championed by the Greek emperor Alexander the Great around 332 B.C., marks a critical point in this region's history. Alexander wanted to combine Greek culture with that of the Middle East, taking ideas, institutions, and administrators from the Egyptians, the Mesopotamians, and the Persians. Although Alexander's vision was never realized, he did leave a lasting impression on the Middle East, as is evident by the cities, public buildings, and monuments throughout the region that bear his name.

Rome was the next major empire to follow, and under Roman rule, commercial cities flourished. Syrians and

Roman ruins at Baalbek, in modern-day Lebanon. By A.D. 120 the Roman Empire ruled most of the area that today is called the Middle East.

Egyptians grew rich from the trade between Europe, Asia, and central Africa. Arab Bedouins prospered in the trade of cloth and spices. Others in the Middle East took to the sea, exploring the Red Sea, the Arabian Gulf, and the Indian Ocean. However, such wealth and prosperity did not come without a price. Roman rule was enforced by a large occupying army, and the **agrarian** communities of the empire were taxed heavily. Furthermore, Rome's leaders showed no tolerance for their subjects' practice of unorthodox religions, an approach that was applied with even greater force once Rome converted to Christianity in the fourth century A.D.

Turks began to migrate to the Middle East in the 10th century. The Seljuk Turks, in particular, advanced westward across Persia (now known as Iran), Mesopotamia, and into Anatolia. Their military success inspired other Turkish tribes to follow, and soon northwestern Iran, northern Iraq, and much of Anatolia became predominantly Turkish.

While the Turks were invading from the east, another group was invading from the west. The Crusaders, sent by the Pope in 1096 to regain Jerusalem for Christianity, stopped the Seljuks from advancing any further and then went on to conquer western Syria and Palestine as well as Jerusalem. The Crusader kingdoms would not last, however, and Muslim warriors forced the last of these Christian knights out of the Middle East by 1291.

Another group of invaders was even more menacing. In the 13th century, the Mongols invaded from the lands north of China. The best-known leader of the Mongols was Genghis Khan. He led his armies to conquer vast areas of central Asia and eastern Persia. His grandson, Kublai Khan, went even further, taking all of Persia and Mesopotamia, including Baghdad.

The Mongols were accustomed to living on the grassy **steppes**. As a result, they saw no need for cities and agriculture, so they destroyed irrigation works in Persia, Mesopotamia, and Syria—an act that had devastating consequences for the people living there.

The Mongols' fierce invasions were halted in 1260. The Mamluks, Turkic slaves who had advanced to high military and political posts in Egypt, banded together and overthrew the Mongols. The Mamluks remained in power in Egypt and Syria until 1517, when they were finally conquered by the Ottoman Turks.

In the late 13th century, a Muslim warrior named Osman began to lead successful raids against Byzantine strongholds in western Anatolia. His followers, known as the Ottomans, spread out in all directions, gaining territories as they went. The Ottomans eventually forged an empire that, at its height, included southeastern Europe, Anatolia, Iraq, western Iran, Greater Syria, Egypt, the western Arabian Peninsula, and the coast of North Africa between

Egypt and eastern Morocco. The Ottoman Empire also conquered vast areas of southeastern Europe, including all of the Balkans, and ruled these areas for centuries. In the 17th century, Ottoman power was still rising, as it threatened Prague and Vienna. Gradually, however, the Ottoman Empire declined. By the end of the 18th century, that decline was accelerated by the advance of the European powers.

Until 1914, European governments preserved peace among themselves by maintaining a balance of power under a loose agreement called the Concert of Europe. No country was willing to let another become the superior power. For the Middle East, this meant that the Ottoman Empire, which became part of the Concert of Europe after the Crimean War in the 1850s, needed to constantly watch the activities of Great Britain, Russia, and Austria. Britain was competing with France, for both empires wanted control of India and saw various territories on the fringes of the Ottoman Empire as useful places to expand their power. This competition went on for decades. Britain fought to remove Napoleon I from Egypt and to depose certain Middle Eastern leaders who were allied with France. Despite Britain's efforts, however, it was France that succeeded in winning a concession from the Egyptian government to build a canal across the *Isthmus* of Suez that would become the Suez Canal.

The pressures that came with constant fighting against the Europeans led the Ottoman leaders to institute changes. In the midst of the battling, Ottoman leaders were exposed to certain Western ideals, and they saw the need for reform in their own lands. At first, the leaders viewed reforms as simply the restoration of the institutions and practices that had originally made their empires so mighty. However, repeated defeat by the Western countries taught these leaders just how necessary reform was.

Initial reform attempts began with the military, although these

This page from a 12th-century Arabic manuscript shows a caravan passing a fortified town. After the death of the Prophet Muhammad in the seventh century, the Arabs spread Islam throughout the Middle East. Arab civilization placed a great importance on education, and during this time the Arabs made great developments in philosophy, medicine, mathematics, science, and literature. The Arab civilization was at its highest point from the 8th to the 13th centuries; after this period, invasions from outside made the Arabs subordinate to various powers.

proved unsuccessful in the beginning. At first, reformers merely duplicated how Western armies equipped and trained their troops, which led many officers to believe they were virtually under the thumb of Western forces. The reformers then realized they should embrace only the Western tactics and policies that were adaptable to Middle Eastern culture. One of the most successful Middle Eastern reformers was Muhammad Ali, an Ottoman officer who led an Albanian regiment sent to Egypt. He gained control of Egypt after Napoleon's forces pulled out in 1801, and, using French advisers and equipment, he developed the region's strongest army and navy. Under his leadership, Egypt became the first Middle Eastern

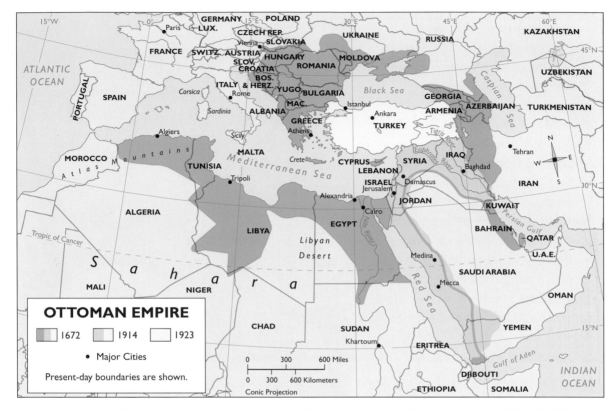

From Turkey, the powerful Ottoman Empire spread throughout the Middle East during the 15th and 16th centuries. By 1672 the empire controlled most of the region that today is known as the Middle East—North Africa, the Arabian Peninsula, and south-central Asia. By the start of World War I (1914) however, the Ottomans' holdings had been reduced by the expansion of the European powers, most notably France and Great Britain. At the end of the war, the Ottoman Empire was dissolved, and its former provinces placed under British or French control.

country to make the transition from subsistence to market agriculture. As the first non-Western ruler to embrace the ideas behind the Industrial Revolution, Muhammad Ali set up **textile** mills and weapons factories with the aid of European advisers. He sent hundreds of his subjects to Europe for technical and military training and brought European instructors to Egypt to teach in the military academies and schools.

WESTERNIZATION, LIBERALISM, AND NATIONALISM

These steps toward Westernization, however, made some groups of the Middle East concerned about where it would eventually lead. Was the Middle East to become merely another region ruled by the Western world? Many people throughout the Middle East eventually began to reject Westernization and wished to create independent, **autonomous** states. In a sense, these people still sought to implement some Western ideas of nationalism and modernity as well, though they did so only to modernize their countries, not to adopt Western culture.

From these newfound ideas came such movements as the National Party in Egypt, the New Ottomans and then the Young Turks in the Ottoman Empire, secret Arab societies in Beirut and Damascus, and the Young Tunisians. For much of the 19th century, these groups and others like them organized, and some fought, against imperial rule—not only against the French and British, but also against the Ottoman Turks. Arab nationalism became popular among intellectuals in Greater Syria, while Armenian nationalism also grew after the massacres of Armenians in Anatolia in the 1890s. Zionism (the movement to reunite the Jewish people in Palestine) had begun to gain momentum in Europe, and the first waves of Jewish settlement in Palestine began in 1882. A Turanian movement stressing the unity and solidarity of the Turkish people from present-day Turkey eastward through Central Asia grew as well.

Most Arabs were still under the reign of the Ottoman Empire, whose leaders were Muslims, but not Arabs. The more remote areas of Arabia were not directly ruled by the Turks, but by tribes representing the Turks, such as the Al Saud, Al Rashid, and others. By the 1880s, France ruled much of North Africa. The Persian Gulf coast was under the imperial protection of Great Britain, as was Egypt and the Sudan. Italy seized Libya in 1911, and Somalia soon thereafter. Persia was semi-independent, with zones of British and Russian influence limiting its **sovereignty**. Also, some peoples in North Africa and the Persian Gulf resisted nationalist movements, preferring to remain under the rule or guidance of Western countries. Those who did support nationalist movements, however, often could not agree among themselves on what should replace imperial rule. Should they revert to previous constitutions or modes of leadership, like monarchies? Should an entirely new form of leadership be established? Debate also raged among people regarding who had the right to make this decision as well as how it would be made. With Middle Eastern peoples divided, Western empires and the Ottomans themselves were able to hold onto their power and influence for longer periods.

World War I (1914–18) brought about the end of the Ottoman Empire and the expansion of British and French influence into the former empire's Arab domains, though that expansion was short-lived. After World War II ended in 1945, their imperial control was essentially at an end.

THE RISE OF ARAB NATIONALISM

The definition of the term *Arab* is trickier than one may think. Some define it culturally, others linguistically, and yet another group racially. The definition of the word has also changed over time. More than 1,500 years ago and earlier, the term was most commonly applied by Aramaic-speaking sedentary dwellers to refer to the pre-literate, nomadic peoples of the Arabian Peninsula. At the time of Muhammad, in the seventh century, an Arab was someone from the Arabian Peninsula. Today, to most people an Arab is a person whose native language is Arabic, a language that was spread from Arabia to much wider areas by the Arab-Islamic conquests of the seventh through the eleventh centuries.

Modern Arab nationalism takes two forms: One, called Pan-

Arabism, refers to the belief that all people who speak Arabic should be united as one nation-state. The second form is more localized, referring to the independence efforts in individual Arabic-speaking countries. Over the last 40 years, this second form of nationalist thinking has become more prevalent, and has also been at the expense of Pan-Arabism.

Four Allied leaders meet outside the Hotel Crillon, Paris, during a post-World War I peace conference in May 1919: from left to right are David Lloyd George, prime minister of Great Britain; Signor Orlando, prime minister of Italy; Georges Clemenceau, prime minister of France; and Woodrow Wilson, president of the United States. After the end of the First World War, the League of Nations was established; this international organization divided much of the Middle East into small states, and granted Great Britain and France mandates to rule them. In theory, the mandate system was intended to prepare the Middle Eastern states for self-government, but in practice the states were little more than French or British colonies.

In 1914, the Ottoman Empire entered World War I on the side of Germany. Britain successfully repulsed Turkish attacks on the Suez Canal and sent forces into Mesopotamia and Palestine. In 1916, Britain promised independence to Hussein ibn Ali, the emir of Mecca and sharif of the Hashemite family, if he would help the Allies against the Ottomans. However, Britain was deliberately vague about how this independence would be recognized. That same year, Hussein, stirred by the Ottoman Empire's suppression of Arabs, announced the beginning of the Arab Revolt. By 1918, the

Oil flows over a derrick at one of the first wells to be drilled in the Middle East, circa 1908. The sale of oil, which began after the end of World War II, soon brought large amounts of money into the region, some of which was used to build modern schools, hospitals, roadways, and government buildings.

combined Arab and British forces drove the Turks from Palestine and Syria.

After World War I, the Arabs expected Britain to grant them independence, and U.S. President Woodrow Wilson urged this action as one of his peace resolution's Fourteen Points. But the British had made arrangements that ran against this course for the Arabs. Most notable was the Balfour Declaration of November 1917, in which the British declared their support for "the establishment in Palestine of a national home for the Jewish people." Britain also made promises to the Kurdish people. But other arrangements that the Allies made among themselves during the war contradicted the original promises to the Arabs, the Kurds, the Zionist Jews, and others. Most important of these was the Sykes-Picot Agreement of 1916. This agreement called for an independent Arab state (it was noted as such on the map accompanying the agreement), but it was never clear how much influence Britain and France expected to maintain over this independent state.

By 1919, the Allies had reached an agreement as to how the Middle East would be divided: Britain would take over Iraq, Palestine, and present-day Jordan, while France would take Syria and Lebanon. In principle, Britain and France were considered mentors that would guide these countries in their development to full independence; in effect, they were supposed to prepare these countries to rule themselves. Thus these acquisitions were officially called mandates, registered under the newly formed League of Nations. The reality, however, was that Britain and France used their position of power to benefit themselves, which the Arabs strongly resented. As it turned out, only in the remote deserts were the Arabs free from Western rule.

In 1920, uprisings in Iraq against British rule compelled the British government to modify the mandate system to create a provisional government. Iraq became formally independent in

1932. In Syria, the French had considerable difficulty in controlling a major national uprising from 1925 to 1927. Despite negotiations in 1938 for increased Syrian autonomy, the Syrians did not achieve full independence until 1946. Jordan obtained partial independence in 1928 and full independence in 1946. Lebanon became independent from France in 1943. Egypt, which had become a British protectorate in 1914, formally became an independent state in 1922. However, British and French influence remained decisive in all these countries until after World War II.

During World War II, Middle Eastern countries found themselves, either by circumstance or by choice, partnered with the Allies or the Axis powers. This had a significant effect on the economies of Middle Eastern countries. For example, in Egypt, the ***industrialization*** trend that had started before the war was developed to the point that by war's end, Egypt was satisfying 86 percent of its domestic needs for certain consumer goods, and manufacturing employed 8.4 percent of the labor force and produced 12 percent of the ***gross domestic product*** (GDP). Iraq experienced an expansion in traditional industries, such as making bricks, processing oilseed, and tanning leather, although no modern factories were built. There were a few improvements in agriculture and the expansion of Iraq's railway system, but these changes were both uncommon in the rest of the Middle East and had only short-term benefits.

Overall, as a result of World War II people in the Middle East had jobs and money—a positive outcome particularly viewed in the aftermath of the Great Depression of the 1930s, which had hit the Middle East very hard. However, there was a shortage of goods on which to spend this new money since, as in the other regions of the world, supplying the huge armies had taken top priority. And while markets expanded and the foreign management of economic and military activities developed further, no positive or lasting impact on the economies of the Middle East actually took place. What would eventually have a tremendous impact on these economies was the discovery of large amounts of oil in the 1920s and 1930s.

It is estimated that the Middle East controls more than 40 percent of the world's oil. Although development of this resource would not occur until after the end of the Second World War, by the 1950s production of oil was bringing large amounts of money into the economies of Iran, Saudi Arabia, and other countries. At first the Western corporations produced the oil, with local leaders getting a share of the wealth; eventually, the countries took over production of the oil themselves, which brought in even more money. The families that ruled in Saudi Arabia, Kuwait, and other lands used the oil wealth to modernize their countries; they also used it to maintain their influence. In 1960, the Organization of Petroleum Exporting Countries (OPEC) was formed. This cartel, which included the major Arab oil-producing states as well as Iran, sets quotas for oil production as a way to control worldwide oil prices.

During World War II, support for Arab unity continued to grow. Leaders made proposals to join together groups of countries: the first proposal was for a union of Syria, Lebanon, Jordan, Palestine, and Iraq; a second was for a union between Egypt and Saudi Arabia. In 1944, a proposal, originally suggested by Great Britain, stated that all sovereign Arab states should be joined into a loose organization. The plan was accepted and the Arab League came into being. That same year, some Arab countries also joined the United Nations. Although the Arab countries voiced commitments to unify with their neighbors, in each of the individual countries those goals were not fully realized. The only goal on which they were united was the resistance against the formation of a Jewish state.

THE CREATION OF ISRAEL AND ITS EFFECT ON THE MIDDLE EAST

After large segments of the Jewish population in Europe were decimated by the Holocaust, the survivors sought out Palestine as a safe haven. However, the Arab majority feared that the flood of refugees pouring in would lead to statehood at the Arabs' expense. In an effort to relieve these fears, during the 1930s Britain had issued "White Papers" in 1933 and 1939. These documents promised to restrict Jewish immigration and land sales to Jews and provide for the establishment of an independent Palestinian state within 10 years. By the end of World War II, Jews in Palestine and the rest of the world increased their demands for a Jewish state. Some groups even resorted to violence, thinking that it would hasten the process.

To a certain degree, the violence did speed things up. Britain announced in 1947 that it was leaving Palestine and called upon the United Nations (UN) to determine Palestine's future. The UN recommended that the area be divided into one state for the Jews, one state for the Arabs, and an internationalized zone around Jerusalem under UN control. Despite unanimous Arab opposition to this proposal, which gave more than half of Palestine to the Jews, the resolution was approved.

On May 14, 1948, the Jewish Agency, which represented the Jewish settlers and their interests, met in Tel Aviv to declare the independent State of Israel, as it was designated by the UN. The United States and the former Soviet Union recognized Israel, as did much of the Western world, but the Arabs rejected this announcement, claiming that their own right to self-determination was being denied. The Arabs in Palestine, with help from Syria and other Arab countries, had already started a civil war in Palestine against the Jews after the enactment of a partition resolution in November 1947. In May 1948, Egypt, Syria, Iraq, Lebanon, and Jordan all declared war against Israel, but they were unable to take control of Palestine. As Jews consolidated control over their portion of Palestine, most Palestinian Arabs fled to neighboring Arab states. As a result, about 450,000 Arab refugees went to areas of Palestine

After the state of Israel was formed in 1948, decades of intermittent fighting with neighboring Arab countries followed. Egypt, the largest of the Arab countries, was one of the primary aggressors. In September 1978, U.S. President Jimmy Carter worked with Egyptian and Israeli leaders during weeks of meetings at the presidential retreat in Camp David, Maryland. The summit was successful, as the two countries agreed to a peace treaty that has persisted. Pictured are Egyptian president Anwar Sadat, Carter, and Israeli prime minister Menachem Begin shaking hands after signing the treaty in 1979.

not under Jewish control, or moved elsewhere in the Arab world, especially Lebanon and Syria.

Despite an **armistice** agreement that the Arab states signed with Israel in 1949, they still refused to recognize the State of Israel, and additional wars followed. In 1956, Britain and France joined Israel against Egypt in a conflict that was primarily waged over control of the Suez Canal. Israel briefly occupied Egypt's Sinai Peninsula in 1956, but it left by the following year. Israel later faced military threats in 1967, but made a pre-emptive attack to begin what was called the Six-Day War, in which it conquered the West Bank, Gaza Strip, Golan Heights, and the Sinai Peninsula (known collectively as the Occupied Territories). Israel fought the Six-Day War with a French-supplied air force and weapons from other European countries. After the Six-Day War, the United States supplied the bulk of weapons to Israel. This aid increased during the 1970s, particularly after the October War in 1973, in which Israel fought against Egypt and Syria. During the 1960s and 1970s, Arab-Israeli disputes were influenced by the global cold war, an ongoing power struggle between the Western powers, led by the United States, and the Communist bloc, led by the former Soviet Union. The Soviet Union supported the Arab states by providing a steady supply of weapons.

In October 1974, the Arab League recognized the Palestine Liberation Organization (PLO), a group that had been founded in 1964 under Egyptian auspices to represent the Palestinian people and work toward official statehood. In addition, the United Nations granted the PLO "observer status," which meant it could participate in UN deliberations but could not vote on resolutions. The 1978 Camp David Accords, under which Israel agreed to return the Sinai Peninsula to Egypt, and the resulting peace treaty between Egypt and Israel in March 1979 removed Egypt from the Arab-Israeli conflict. Israel and Jordan also signed a peace treaty in October 1994. But Israel has yet to reach peace agreements with the other Arab states, or a resolution of the Palestinian problem. In December 1987, a movement known as the *intifada*—a series of demonstrations, riots, and strikes against Israeli rule—began in the Gaza Strip and spread to the West Bank.

THE ISLAMIC REVOLUTION IN IRAN

While violence and strife were occurring between the Arab states and Israel, discord was also brewing in Iran during the late

In 1979, the pro-U.S. government of Iran was overthrown and replaced by a strict Islamic regime headed by the Ayatollah Khomeini. In this photo of a 1979 demonstration, soldiers and others carry posters of Khomeini. The Iranian Revolution sparked unrest in other parts of the Middle East, as Khomeini tried to encourage Islamist movements in other countries.

1970s. During the 1960s and 1970s, Iran's ruler, Mohammad Reza Shah Pahlavi, tried to modernize the country at great speed—a process he called the White Revolution. Living standards rose, women were given the right to vote and other civil liberties, land reform took place, and education improved. But **inflation** soared, and mass migration to cities as the economy became more industrialized disrupted Iran's traditional social structure. The shah faced opposition from radical nationalists, labor union leaders,

Marxists, intellectuals, and students who called for change. Iran's political development had not kept a fast enough pace with its economic change, and the shah reacted against this opposition by becoming more repressive. Imprisonment, torture, and even death at the hands of the shah's agents became common.

The most popular leaders of the opposition to the shah were primarily Muslim clerics. One of these was the Shiite leader Ayatollah Ruhollah Khomeini, who had been forced into exile during the 1960s for criticizing the shah over giving women the vote, among other things. Khomeini broadcasted messages to his followers from exile in Iraq, and later from Paris. Opposition to the shah grew in strength and in 1978 hundreds of demonstrators were killed in clashes with the police. In January 1979, the shah left Iran to receive medical treatment in the United States. He would never return. Khomeini's followers overthrew the government, leading to the ayatollah's return, and Khomeini and his supporters set up the Islamic Republic of Iran in April 1979.

The Iranian Revolution proved to influence events beyond its borders. In neighboring Iraq, dictator Saddam Hussein feared that the Iranian Revolution would prompt Iraqi Shiite Muslims in his country to rebel. Using a border dispute as a pretext, in September 1980 Hussein invaded Iran. In 1988, the two countries finally accepted a UN resolution calling for a cease-fire. Other Gulf states, particularly Bahrain and Kuwait, feared that Khomeini would attempt to "export" the Shiite revolution to their countries. In 1981 six states—Oman, Saudi Arabia, Bahrain, Kuwait, Qatar, and the United Arab Emirates—formed the Gulf Cooperation Council (GCC), an organization that would provide for mutual defense if one of its members was attacked. The GCC nations tried to remain neutral during the Iran-Iraq War, but eventually supported Iraq after Iranian attacks on their oil tankers.

The rise of a fundamentalist Islamic regime in Iran inspired efforts to establish Islamist governments in other countries as well. In Egypt, President Anwar Sadat, who had signed the peace agreement with Israel and forged ties to the West, was assassinated in 1981; his successor, Hosni Mubarak, spent much of the 1990s cracking down on fundamentalist opposition groups such as the Muslim Brotherhood. In Algeria, fighting between the government and supporters of a banned Islamist political party began in 1992, leading to a civil war that lasted more than 10 years and killed more than 100,000 people.

THE GULF WAR AND ITS AFTERMATH

In August 1990, Saddam Hussein once again used an imaginary threat to precipitate war. The Iraqi economy had been severely weakened by the long war with Iran, and the population was starting to blame the dictator. To divert attention from his domestic problems, Saddam directed his forces to invade and annex Kuwait, blaming this neighboring country for its part in decreasing the international price of oil. In response, a coalition led by the United States launched the Gulf War against Iraq in January 1991. After a campaign of aerial bombing and a brief ground war, the coalition defeated Iraqi forces by the end of February and liberated Kuwait. The coalition powers expected Saddam to fall from power in Baghdad, but he did not. After the Gulf War, economic sanctions remained in effect against Iraq because it did not fulfill its obligation to destroy all its nuclear, chemical, and biological weapons.

At the end of the Gulf War, the governments of the United States and the Soviet Union jointly sponsored a historic meeting between Israel, Syria, Lebanon, Jordan, and the Palestinians. The Madrid Conference, held in October–November 1991, was intended to create a framework for peace in the Middle East. The conference led to the 1994 Israel-Jordan peace agreement. It also was the catalyst for secret talks between Israeli and Palestinian negotiators in Norway

Yasir Arafat, the leader of the Palestine Liberation Organization (PLO), shakes hands with Israeli prime minister Yitzhak Rabin as President Bill Clinton watches on the White House lawn on September 13, 1993. During the 1990s, Israel and the Palestinian Arabs seemed to be making progress toward ending their long-running struggle and creating an autonomous Palestinian state; however, after Arafat rejected a final Israeli peace plan in the fall of 2000, the situation deteriorated into violence once again.

during 1993. These meetings led to a resolution that, it was hoped, would result in an end to Israeli-Palestinian violence. The goals of the Oslo Accords, which were signed in a September 1993 ceremony at the White House, were the ultimate removal of Israeli troops from the occupied territories of the West Bank and Gaza Strip and the establishment of Palestinian self-rule in those areas. A governmental entity called the Palestinian Authority, led by PLO head

Yasir Arafat, was recognized by Israel as the legitimate representative of the Palestinians.

An interim agreement was signed in 1995 at a second White House ceremony, giving control of a number of cities and communities to the Palestinian Authority, while permitting Israeli settlements in the West Bank and Gaza Strip to remain. A final peace agreement was scheduled for the fall of 2000. However, during a meeting with U.S. President Bill Clinton at Camp David, the Palestinian leadership rejected an Israeli proposal for the creation of the autonomous Palestinian state. Soon after, a second *intifada* began. As the death toll rose on both sides, the prospects for peace dimmed.

During the 1990s, the United States continued to maintain a military presence in the Middle East, stationing troops in Saudi Arabia, Kuwait, and other countries. In 1992 U.S. troops were sent to Somalia, hard hit by famine and internal strife, as part of a humanitarian mission; after an attempt to capture a hostile Somali warlord resulted in the deaths of 18 Marines, the U.S. forces were withdrawn from the country.

In March 2003, tensions between Iraq and the United States escalated into another war. President George W. Bush ordered U.S. forces to lead an international coalition in an invasion of Iraq. Responding to reports that President Saddam Hussein was storing deadly weapons in the country, the coalition overthrew the dictator.

THE MIDDLE EAST TODAY

The Middle East today is still a region beset by many conflicts. Secular nationalism competes with Islam-based governance as the leading ideology. National borders, often created by the Western world to serve its own interests, do not typically reflect natural borders. None of the Arab states is a democracy, and the economic development of these countries, except those with large oil reserves, is often stunted. Population growth is very high, challenging

Women cast ballots in an election for local representatives in Oman. Although there are no democracies among the Arab countries of the Middle East, in recent years more liberal countries such as Bahrain, Oman, and Qatar have allowed popular election of some leaders.

governments to supply enough education, health care, and jobs to the expanding adult populations. In particular, educational systems are antiquated in many countries, as indicated by the low levels of scientific and technical expertise exhibited by workers.

As a result of these difficult circumstances, many people in the Arab countries do not like their governments, who have reason to fear popular unrest and a lack of loyalty. In many countries, radical and violent opposition movements have taken shape and Arab terrorism directed against the West has incubated. Many Middle Easterners dislike the foreign friends and sponsors of governments; foremost among this group of enemies is the United States.

In Iran, there is great and mounting discontent with the Islamic Republic. The Iranian people, under very restrictive election laws, voted for reformer President Mohammed Khatemi, but the real power in the country resides with Khomeini's successor, Ayatollah Seyyed Ali Khamanei. The Iranian government has had very bad relations with the United States since 1979, yet the people of Iran today are among the most pro-American in the world.

Nonetheless, there have been successful democratic movements in the Middle East. Israel and Turkey are democracies, and have been gradually integrated into the world economy. Some Arab countries, such as Jordan, Morocco, Tunisia, Bahrain, and Qatar, have made progress toward economic self-sufficiency and political liberalization.

Five times each day, a *muezzin* calls Muslims to prayer from the minaret of the Koutubia Mosque in Marrakech. Approximately 95 percent of the people of the Middle East are Muslims.

The Countries of the Middle East

*T*his chapter presents a brief overview of the countries in the Middle East, including some history and information on the economy and politics of each. For more detailed, in-depth information, readers are encouraged to turn to the books covering individual countries in the MODERN MIDDLE EAST NATIONS series.

ALGERIA

Algeria has been ruled by distant empires for much of its history. From 1400 to 1830, a power vacuum in Algeria led to a period of lawless piracy along the Barbary Coast. In 1830, the French army invaded Algeria to end the piracy and make the country a French colony. After a century of French rule, Algeria fought a brutal war for independence, ultimately becoming an independent nation in 1962. Today Algeria is ruled by a military government, and the president acts as a virtual dictator. There is a 389-member legislative house, called the National People's Assembly, but it is not very powerful.

Prior to achieving independence, the Algerian economy was dependent on agriculture. Today, oil and natural gas are the backbone of the economy. Algeria has the fifth-largest reserves of natural gas in the world, is fourteenth in the world in oil reserves, and is the second-largest gas exporter. Algeria could be one of the wealthiest nations in Africa if political turmoil did not constantly rack its economy. The civil war of the 1990s particularly frustrated economic growth, and large-scale unemployment and poor living standards still plague the country.

BAHRAIN

Bahrain is one of the smallest countries in the Arabian Gulf. Its size, combined with its central location in the Gulf region, requires it to play a delicate balancing act in affairs with its larger neighbors.

The country of Bahrain (which is actually composed of 33 islands) first garnered attention in approximately 3000 B.C. when it became the center of the great trading empire of the Dilmun civilization. The Al Khalifa family, the ruling family of Bahrain, arrived in the mid-18th century. Prior to the Al Khalifa's reign, Bahrain was occupied by the Persians, the Omanis, the Portuguese, and the British. Today, Bahrain, still ruled by the Al Khalifa, has a constitutional monarchy whereby the mantle of king, or emir, automatically passes from father to eldest son. The emir appoints the prime minister as well as the cabinet.

Because Bahrain was the first Arab Gulf state to discover oil (in 1932), it was also the first to enjoy the benefits that came with oil revenues, namely a significant improvement in the quality of education and health care for its citizens. The oil reserves of Bahrain are small when compared to other Arab countries, but the country's leaders have used oil profits wisely to build national revenue. Over the decades, Bahrain has slowly diversified its economy, thus making sure it has a firm foundation when the country's reserves are exhausted. However, there are still problems that Bahrain's government must address. Unemployment, especially among the young, and the depletion of underground water resources are both long-term economic problems. And the ongoing quarrel between the country's ruling family and poor Shiite Muslims has remained a political issue.

DJIBOUTI

Djibouti, located on the Horn of Africa between Ethiopia and Somalia, has been a land of nomads since its very beginning. The two primary tribes are the Afars and the Issas. In 1888, French Somaliland was established, and Djibouti became its official capital in 1892. Independence and the reunification of Somalia in the late 20th century inspired anticolonialism movements in Djibouti. The first territorial assembly was established in 1957. France, however, was slow to grant the territory independence. In 1977, the French finally agreed that the Territory of the Afars and the Issas would become the independent Republic of Djibouti.

Djibouti is ruled by a republican government. The current president is Ismael Omar Guelleh. The president appoints the prime minister as well as the Council of Ministers. The legislative branch consists of the **unicameral**, 65-member Chamber of Deputies, whose members are elected by popular vote for five-year terms.

The economy of Djibouti is based on service activities related to the country's strategic position as a free-trade zone in northeast Africa. Djibouti provides services as both a transit port for the region and as an international transshipment and refueling center. Because this country has few natural resources and little industry, it is heavily dependent upon foreign assistance to help support its balance of payments and to finance development projects.

Civil war, a high population growth rate, and an influx of refugees caused by regional wars have led to economic difficulties that Djibouti is still struggling with today, namely, high unemployment, long-term external debts, and decreased port activity now that Ethiopia has more trade-route options.

Egypt

It is impossible to think of Egypt without thinking of the ancient pyramids, but this country has made a reputation for itself in modern times as well. In theory, Egypt has a republican form of government with executive, legislative, and judicial branches, though in practice the government does not maintain a balance of power like other republican governments do. The president is nominated by the People's Assembly for a six-year term, and the nomination must then be validated by a national, popu-

This view of downtown Cairo includes the Sultan Hassan Mosque. Cairo is Egypt's capital and is one of the largest cities in the Middle East.

lar referendum. A prime minister is then appointed by the president. Egypt has a military-bureaucratic government, and the president rules as a virtual dictator. The parliament has very little power.

A rapidly growing population (the largest in the Arab world), limited **arable** land, and dependence on the Nile all continue to overtax resources and generally make Egyptians anxious about the future. The Egyptian government has attempted to remedy this situation through economic reforms and massive investment in communications and physical infrastructure. Currently, oil represents about 50 percent of Egypt's export earnings. Cotton is the second most-important export.

Through the 1990s, Egypt succeeded in reducing inflation and budget deficits and in increasing foreign reserves. Steps towards a more market-oriented economy have also prompted an increase in foreign investment. A continued oil-price recovery, a moderate rebound in tourism, and an increase in gas exports indicate that the Egyptian economy is poised for future growth.

IRAN

Known as Persia before 1935, Iran became an Islamic republic in 1979 after the ruling shah was forced into exile. Officially, Iran is known as the Islamic Republic of Iran, and it ranks among the world's leaders in its reserves of oil and natural gas.

During 1980–88, Iran fought a bloody war with Iraq, which began when Iraq invaded the country. Key issues affecting the country today include widespread demands for reform, the pace at which modernization is accomplished, and a reconciliation between an autocracy of clerics and a system of popular government.

Until 1906, Iran was ruled as a monarchy under a shah, or sovereign leader. In 1906, a popular revolution forced the shah to accept a constitution that limited his powers. Beginning in the early

1950s, popular disaffection with arbitrary rule grew until it culminated in the 1979 Islamic Revolution. Today, Iran is ruled by a **theocratic** republic in which the executive, legislative, and judicial branches are separate and can check one another's exercise of power. The chief of state is the president, who is elected by popular vote to a four-year term. He can appoint as many vice presidents as he wants and also selects members of the Council of Ministers. The council, however, must be approved by the legislative branch, the unicameral Islamic Consultative Assembly.

Iran's economy is a mixture of central planning, state ownership of oil and other large-scale enterprises, village agriculture, and small-scale private trading and service ventures. Historically, agriculture has been the most important sector of Iran's economy, but the mining sector, which is dominated by the production of oil, has experienced rapid growth since Iran nationalized its oil fields in the 1950s. Iran still is struggling to diversify its economy and encourage foreign investment.

IRAQ

In recent years Iraq has been at the forefront of the news and in current events because of the activities of its dictator, Saddam Hussein, whose regime was overthrown in April 2003. Iraq became an independent nation in 1932, but was not free from a strong British influence until 1958, when a military **coup** overthrew the Hashemite monarchy. Saddam was a leader of the Baath Party, which overthrew Iraq's government in 1968, and he remained an important behind-the-scenes power until becoming president of Iraq in 1979.

The economy of modern-day Iraq is based on oil, which has traditionally provided about 95 percent of the country's export earnings. Four major factors have affected the Iraqi economy since 1980. First, there was the war with Iran for most of the 1980s. Then, there was the international oil oversupply in the 1980s and

1990s, which caused a drop in oil prices, and in turn Iraq's revenue from oil fell. Third, Iraq was subjected to UN economic sanctions following its invasion of Kuwait in 1990 and the Gulf War, in which it fought against a U.S.-led coalition. Finally, the Iraqi economy has also been crushed by the destruction of the country's basic infrastructure and its financial bankruptcy.

In 2002 and early 2003, the United States and other UN countries received reports that Saddam Hussein possessed weapons of mass destruction. The administration of President George W. Bush responded aggressively, and in March, the United States and Great Britain invaded Iraq, quickly dismantled Saddam's regime, and installed a provisional authority. Although there were continual guerilla attacks throughout the rest of the year, coalition forces aimed to hand power back to the Iraqi people by the summer of 2004.

ISRAEL

Israel was formed in 1948 as a Jewish state in the historic region of Palestine. The country's history is based on an ancient Jewish connection to the region, a recurrent theme in Jewish tradition and writing since the second millennium B.C. The fact that it is a Jewish state surrounded by Arab and predominately Islamic countries has influenced its politics, its economy, its foreign relations, and even its demography.

The history of Israel has been a history of war. Immediately after declaring independence, Israel was attacked by Egypt, Jordan, Syria, Lebanon, and Iraq. A truce ended the fighting in 1949, but tension and hostility remained. As a result of the Six-Day War of 1967, Israel occupied the Sinai Peninsula, the Golan Heights, the West Bank, and the Gaza Strip. In that same year, Israel also captured mostly Arab East Jerusalem (the mostly Jewish West Jerusalem has been part of Israel from the beginning). Israel now

Jewish worshippers face the Western Wall, or Wailing Wall, in Jerusalem. The wall—all that remains of the second Jewish temple, which was destroyed by the Romans in A.D. 70—has great symbolic importance to Jews from all over the world.

claims the entire city as its capital. Today, clashes and violence still erupt between Jews and Arabs in the region, and Israel appears to be a nation far from peace.

Israel is a multiparty, parliamentary republic with ultimate authority vested by the people in the legislature, known as the Knesset. There is no written constitution, but a number of basic laws passed by the parliament over the decades determine government operations and activities. Furthermore, some of the functions of a constitution are filled by the Declaration of Establishment and the Israeli citizenship law.

Economically, the challenges of national security and immigration have been great for Israel. The economic burden of the military fosters dependence on foreign military aid, particularly from the United States. Furthermore, political conflict keeps Israel economically isolated from much of the Middle East. However, on the plus side, the constant influx of people with many different skills and backgrounds contributes to Israel's economic well-being. Both factors have stimulated the drive to create a successful industrial economy that can afford to maintain infrastructure and continue services. Today, Israel has a technologically advanced market economy with substantial government participation. Despite limited natural resources, Israel has intensively developed its agricultural and industrial sectors over the past 20 years and is largely self-sufficient in food production except for grains.

JORDAN

The Kingdom of Jordan has an ancient history, as do most of the countries of the Arab world. Its modern history, however, dates from 1921, when Emir Abdullah, son of Sharif Hussein, established the Emirate of Jordan as a self-governing territory under British mandate. In May 1946, Emir Abdullah was proclaimed king of the independent Hashemite Kingdom of Jordan. King Abdullah was assassinated in 1950, and his son, Talal, became king. But Talal was deposed after just one year in office because of mental illness, and his son, Hussein became king. King Hussein is perhaps Jordan's best-known ruler as a result of his efforts to achieve peace in the Middle East. During his reign, Jordan signed a peace agreement

Pedestrians walk past buildings in Kuwait City, the largest city in Kuwait. Like the people of several other Gulf states, Kuwait's population is made up of more foreign workers than Kuwaiti citizens.

with Israel. Following Hussein's death in 1999, his eldest son, Abdullah II, assumed the throne.

Jordan is a constitutional monarchy. The constitution was first proclaimed on January 8, 1952, and since then has been amended several times to meet the country's changing needs. The king rules the country, and although there is a parliament made up of both appointed and elected representatives, it has little power.

Jordan is a small county with a limited supply of water. Debt, poverty, and unemployment have been chronic problems. However, Jordan's educational system and medical infrastructure are among the best in the Middle East. Since assuming the throne in 1999, King Abdullah II has pushed broad economic reforms in an effort to improve the living standards of his people.

Because of its small size, Jordan has often found itself buffeted by the goings-on between its larger, more powerful neighbors. In 1950, the union between Jordan and the West Bank was formally declared. However, when Israel occupied the West Bank in 1967, Jordan's industrial production declined by about 20 percent. The agricultural sector suffered an even harsher blow, since the West Bank contained almost half of all of Jordan's agricultural land. In 1974, the Arab League declared the West Bank the rightful land of the Palestine Liberation Organization, and in 1988 Jordan formally renounced its claim to the area.

KUWAIT

The genesis of modern-day Kuwait began in the middle of the 18th century, when members of the Bani Utub clan moved to the area from the central region of the Arabian Peninsula. Kuwait was a British protectorate from 1899 until 1961, when it became independent under Sheikh Abdullah al-Salem al-Sabah.

Kuwait is governed by a nominal constitutional monarchy. According to the constitution, which is based on a combination of presidential and parliamentary systems, the government is based on a separation of powers. The emir and the National Assembly have legislative authority, and the emir, the cabinet, and the ministers have executive authority. In reality, the emir rules the country and the parliament has only symbolic authority.

Iraqi allegations that Kuwait was deliberately overproducing oil were the grounds on which Saddam Hussein invaded this small country in 1990. The unwarranted invasion convinced the U.S. to lead an international coalition in an assault that started the Persian Gulf War. After the war, Kuwait spent more than $160 billion to rebuild its infrastructure.

Kuwait is an oil-rich country. Petroleum accounts for nearly half of the GDP, 90 percent of export revenues, and 75 percent of government income. By law, 10 percent of all oil revenues is deposited in a special reserve fund to provide for the day when oil reserves are exhausted. The government uses oil revenues to provide health care, education, municipal services, and public utilities.

LEBANON

When it first emerged as an independent state in 1943, Lebanon appeared to have everything it needed for success. Its strategic location and relatively stable government made it a major trade and financial center. However, there was an imbalance of power between the minority Maronite Christians, who controlled the government, and Muslims, who felt excluded from government although they were the majority group. In 1975, civil war broke out in Lebanon between Muslim and Christian groups. Although Syrian occupation resulted in an April 1976 cease-fire, the violence and attacks continued for the next 15 years.

Lebanon is ruled by a republican system of government, and the current president is Emile Lahoud. There is also a prime minister, a cabinet, and a unicameral National Assembly. Prior to 1990, an

A Lebanese man contemplates the rushing Asai River, in the Bekaa Valley near Hormel. Lebanon was once the most cosmopolitan country of the Middle East; today it continues to recover from a devastating 16-year-long civil war.

unwritten agreement known as the National Pact specified that the president had to be a Maronite Christian, the prime minister had to be a Sunni Muslim, the speaker of parliament had to be a Shia Muslim, and the chief of staff of the armed forces had to be a Druze (another Islamic sect).

The 1975–91 civil war in Lebanon seriously damaged its infrastructure, cutting the country's national output by half. The country also lost its status as an international banking hub. Since then, Lebanon has succeeded in rebuilding much of its physical and financial infrastructures, partly in thanks to "Horizon 2000," the government's $20-billion reconstruction program. However, serious challenges remain. The country's reconstruction was financed primarily by loans from domestic banks. Furthermore, the government has been unable to control the growth of the country's massive debt. Without large-scale international aid and rapid privatization of state-owned enterprises, markets may force a currency devaluation and debt default. Most important, although Syria has intervened less in Lebanon since the civil war, there is no certainty that it will not meddle in domestic affairs again. As long as the issues of security and foreign policy remain unresolved, Lebanon will be a dependency of Syria.

LIBYA

Libya is perhaps best known today for its dictator, Muammar Qaddafi. His particular brand of politics—a blend of socialism and Islam that he calls the Third International Theory—has supported **subversives** and terrorists all over the world for the sake of bringing an end to Marxism and capitalism. In theory, the type of government in Libya is *Jamahiriya* (a state of the masses), which refers to governance by the populace through local councils. The reality, however, is that Libya is a country ruled by a military dictatorship.

Qaddafi came to power in September 1969 when he led a revolutionary group of army officers in overthrowing the royal government and establishing his own. Under his leadership, Libya has taken a more active role in Middle Eastern and international affairs.

Libya and U.S. relations have been strained even at the best of times. In 1981, U.S. Navy jets shot down two Libyan fighter planes over the Gulf of Sidra. In March 1986, another encounter in the gulf resulted in the destruction of two Libyan ships by U.S. Navy ships. In 1992, the U.S. accused Libya of manufacturing chemical weapons, and the United Nations imposed sanctions against Libya for refusing to **extradite** the two terrorists suspected in the 1988 bombing of Pan American Flight 103 over Lockerbie, Scotland. In 1999, Libya finally agreed to hand over the two suspects. However, Libya remains on a U.S. list of countries that sponsor international terrorism.

Although Libya has one of the highest per capita GDP in Africa, little of this income is held by the common people. Import restrictions and inefficient resource allocations have led to periodic shortages of resources. While the economy depends primarily on revenues from oil, agriculture remains the main occupation of the Libyan people. However, erratic rainfall often causes irrigation problems.

MAURITANIA

The African country of Mauritania, known officially as the Islamic Republic of Mauritania, became a fully independent country in 1960. Prior to independence, it was ruled by the French. Mauritania is dominated by the Maures—descendants of Arab and Berber nomads. It is one of the few places in the world where slavery is still practiced, and violence between the Maures in the north and black Africans in the south is common.

Mauritania is ruled by a republican government. The constitution approved in 1991 provides for an executive president, elected for a six-year term, and a bicameral legislature, consisting of a national assembly and a senate. The president appoints the prime ministers.

The Mauritanian economy is primarily ***pastoral*** and is heavily dependent upon foreign aid. Mining and fishing are two industries that are becoming more prominent in the economy. Mauritania has extensive deposits of iron ore, and its coastal waters are among the richest fishing areas in the world. However, a decline in the world demand for iron ore and overexploitation of the coastal waters by foreigners threaten these important sources of revenue.

MOROCCO

Prior to World War II, Morocco was divided between France and Spain. During World War II, the heads of the Allied government used Casablanca as an important meeting place. Morocco became independent in 1956. Today the country is ruled by a constitutional monarchy, which was established after France and Spain agreed to recognize Moroccan independence. The country has a hereditary monarchy, and the king acts as the head of state and commander-in-chief of the armed forces. He appoints the prime minister and cabinet and can dissolve the Chamber of Representatives, which is the country's legislature. Although the king still has great power in Morocco, local and regional governments are stronger here than in other Arab countries, and political liberalization is underway, though it is unfolding at a moderate pace.

Agriculture forms the basis of Morocco's economy. The country faces challenges typical of developing countries: restraining government spending, reducing constraints on private activities and foreign trade, and achieving sustainable economic growth. In 1999 and 2000, drought conditions led to a rather stagnant economy. Since then, favorable rainfalls have led Morocco to anticipate future economic growth.

OMAN

Unlike many Arab countries that achieved independence during the 20th century, Oman's independence is generally thought to have begun in 1650, when the Portuguese were expelled from the country. Omani commercial power also expanded significantly at this time, setting the stage for Oman to become a trading partner with the European community. Throughout most of the 18th, 19th, and 20th centuries, Oman was under strong British influence.

Oman is a country that has only recently attempted full-scale modernization. Since coming to power in 1970, Sultan Qaboos bin Said Al Bu Said implemented a modernization program that opened Oman to the rest of the world. In Oman the sultan has multiple positions as the head of state; prime minister; and minister of foreign affairs, finance, and defense. A Council of Ministers carries out the administrative and legal functions of the government, and a consultative council (*Majlis al-Shura*) helps shape social, economic, and educational policies.

Prior to the discovery and exploitation of oil and natural gas in the Sultanate of Oman in the mid-1960s, the economy relied primarily on fishing, agriculture, and traditional crafts such as boat-making. Oman's economy today maintains a largely traditional sector based on agriculture as well as a modern sector based on oil. The government controls the oil and gas sector and, therefore, much of the economy. The government has also encouraged job growth in the private sector to reduce unemployment.

QATAR

Ruled by the Al Thani family since the mid-1800s, Qatar (pronounced "cutter" or "gutter") has over the past half-century transformed itself from a poor British protectorate known only for pearling into an independent state with significant oil and gas revenues.

During the time of the Prophet Muhammad, the people of the Qatar Peninsula were known for weaving fine striped cloth and forging excellent spears. By the 16th century, however, the peninsula may have become uninhabited, as historians have concluded from a lack of evidence dating from the period. After Arab tribes moved back into Qatar, it became a British protectorate. This relationship endured until 1971, when Britain decided to withdraw from the Gulf region. Today, Qatar is ruled by a traditional monarchy. The emir decrees laws upon the recommendation of the Council of Ministers and the Advisory Council.

Like other countries in the Middle East, oil plays a large role in Qatar's economy. Qatar has the third-largest oil reserves in the world, and its standard of living is comparable with that of most industrialized Western European countries. Production and export of natural gas are becoming increasingly important, and long-term economic goals include the development of offshore petroleum and the diversification of the economy. Qatar has been more liberal than many of its Gulf Arab neighbors. Since 1996, the independent Al-Jazeera television network has become the most popular media outlet in the Arab world owing to the success of programs on which controversial issues are debated openly.

SAUDI ARABIA

The history of modern-day Saudi Arabia began in 1902, when Abdul Aziz al-Saud and his followers captured the city of Riyadh and reclaimed control of it for his family. In 1924, the Al Saud took the Hejaz away from the Hashemite family and assumed control of Mecca and Medina, the two cities held most sacred by Muslims. In 1933, the lands controlled by Abdul Aziz became officially known as the Kingdom of Saudi Arabia. From 1953, when Abdul Aziz died, to 1970, when King Faisal took power, Saudi Arabia continued to establish itself as a leading financial power in the Islamic world and as a major oil producer in the international economy.

Saudi Arabia has a hereditary monarchy; the king is Fahd bin Abd al-Aziz al-Saud. However, since King Fahd had a stroke in the mid-1990s, the de facto ruler has been his half-brother, Crown Prince Abdullah bin Abdul Aziz al-Saud.

The economy is dominated by oil. Saudi Arabia has the largest reserves of petroleum in the world, is the largest exporter of petroleum, and has a leading role in OPEC. Because of the importance of Mecca and Medina to Muslims, Saudi Arabia also has an important role as the spiritual center of Islam.

SOMALIA

Somalia was first conquered by the Arabs, then colonized by Britain and Italy, and finally granted independence in 1960. Today

Somalia consists of the territory that was British Somaliland, which became independent on June 26, 1960, and Italian Somaliland, which became independent on July 1 of that same year.

In 1969, a group of military officers led by General Siad Barre seized power and proclaimed a **socialist** regime. Barre's regime was ousted in January 1991, and turmoil, fighting, and **anarchy** followed for nine years. Today Somalia, although ruled by Chief of State Abulkassim Salat Hassan, has no observed central authority due to interclan fighting and banditry.

Somalia is one of the world's poorest and least developed countries, and it has few resources. Much of the economy was devastated by civil war, and there have been no real attempts to diversify any income-generating activities. Ongoing civil strife in Mogadishu, the capital, and outlying areas has obstructed all significant economic

To the West, Saudi Arabia is known primarily for its vast oil reserves; the large country on the Arabian Peninsula exports more oil than any other country in the world. To Muslims, however, Saudi Arabia is more important as the location of the two holiest sites in Islam, the cities of Mecca and Medina. Millions of Muslims make the pilgrimage to Mecca each year.

advances and has not allowed for international aid arrangements. The country has been relying on livestock activities in the north and agricultural products in the south to generate income. However, Somalia's economic future remains insecure.

SUDAN

In ancient times Egypt dominated Sudan; in later periods the Romans, the Arabs, the Ottoman Turks, and the British all held power over Sudan as well. During the first half of the 20th century Egypt and Britain shared control of Sudan, an arrangement that finally ended in 1953. The country officially became independent in 1956. Since then, however, problems have plagued Sudan. Cultural differences between the Arab peoples in the north and the black African peoples in the south erupted into civil war after independence was granted. Today, war and famine still plague Sudan. Between 1,000 and 2,000 displaced people per day arrive seeking assistance at the centers operated by international relief organizations.

Currently, the government of Sudan is in transition. A ruling military *junta* took power in 1989, but the government is dominated by members of Sudan's National Islamic Front (NIF), a fundamentalist political organization that uses the National Congress Party (NCP) as its legal front. Omar al-Bashir controls the government as president.

Sudan has a poor economy—not surprising given its history of civil war, chronic instability, bad weather, and counterproductive economic policies. In 1999, Sudan began exporting oil. The growth of the oil industry, coupled with agricultural improvements, should ensure some measure of future economic growth.

SYRIA

Syria is a land that has been inhabited since ancient times, although the modern independent state of Syria was not established until 1946. Syria has a republican form of government, but has been ruled by a succession of Baath Party military governments since March 1963. The president (who must be a Muslim according to the constitution) appoints ministers of his own choosing to make up the executive branch. The legislative branch is made up of the People's Council.

Syria is a relatively new country in an old land, a situation reflected by its economy. It wasn't until the 1960s that Syrian manufacturing began to grow significantly. Textile production is the largest single manufacturing industry in Syria. However, Syrian

A row of Ghorfas, fortified buildings where grain and olive oil were stored, in Ksar Ouled, Tunisia. The Berber residents of Tunisia built these Ghorfas more than 600 years ago.

artisans are famous for their silk brocades and rugs and for their artistry in copper, silver, brass, and steel metalwork.

Even though a large hydroelectric plant was built at the Euphrates Dam in the late 1970s, the supply of electricity is a constant problem in Syria. Many places can count on being without power for up to four hours a day.

Syria is a very heterogeneous society. Sunni Muslims form the majority, but the minority Alawite community has dominated the government since 1966. There are also many Christians, Druze and other Muslim sects, and a small minority of Jews in Syria.

TUNISIA

In ancient times, the Tunisian city of Carthage was the largest and strongest of the Phoenician settlements. After the fall of Carthage the region of present-day Tunisia was successively ruled by Romans, Vandals (a Teutonic tribe), Arabs, Turks, and the French.

Organized resistance to French rule first took place in 1954, and over the next several years Tunisia gained its independence in gradual stages. France would give Tunisia as little autonomy as it could get away with, for a time placating the Tunisians while still retaining power over them. Tunisians continued to demand more independence. Finally, in 1956–57 Tunisia succeeded in becoming an independent republic.

As in many other Arab countries, the National Assembly of Tunisia acts basically as a façade for democracy. Today General Zine el-Abidine Ben Ali, who seized power in 1987, essentially rules Tunisia as a dictator.

Tunisia has a diverse economy, with significant agricultural, mining, energy, tourism, and manufacturing sectors. Governmental control of economic affairs, while still heavy, has gradually lessened over the past decade with increasing privatization, simplification of the tax structure, and a prudent approach to debt. Inflation has been curtailed, and improved tourism and increased trade have been key elements in the steady economic growth Tunisia is now experiencing. Broader privatization, further liberalization of the investment code to increase foreign ventures, and improvements in government efficiency are among the country's objectives.

TURKEY

Turkey was created in 1923 from the Turkish remnants of the Ottoman Empire. The Turkish republic was founded on six basic principles incorporated into the constitution: republicanism, Turkish nationalism, **populism**, secularism, statism (state intervention or complete control of economic sectors), and revolutionism (an approach to instituting changes in full and at once).

Unfortunately, the years following World War II saw Turkey plagued by severe economic and social strains and increasing political discontent. A second constitution was adopted in 1961, but a series of ever-weaker governments caused Turkey to slide into chaos and violence between extremist groups. Another constitution was implemented in 1982, which was an important step toward bringing Turkey back under civilian rule.

In the years since then, Turkey has had to struggle with internal strife, a weak economy, political scandals, and conflicts with other nations. Matters were not helped when in August 1999, a massive earthquake struck, killing at least 15,000 people and injuring over 30,000. The government's relief efforts during the crisis prompted harsh criticism from the people, many of whom thought the response was too slow and that the government should not have used inept contractors to raise substandard housing in the first place.

Turkey is governed by a republican parliamentary democracy. Essentially, legislative power rests in the National Assembly. This is a 550-member unicameral body, the members of which are direct-ly elected to five-year terms. The head of government is the prime minister, who represents the majority party or coalition in parliament. The president, as chief of state, is chosen by parliament for a seven-year term. Unlike most other Middle Eastern countries, however, Turkey is a democracy, although its military still has much influence over the country's affairs.

Turkey's economy, as previously mentioned, has been marked by erratic growth and serious imbalances. The government has a great deal of influence over the Turkish economy and still plays a major role in basic industry, banking, transport, and communication. The most important industry, and the largest exporter, is textiles and clothing, which is almost entirely under private control. The future of Turkey's economy is looking good, with strong financial support from the IMF, a tighter fiscal policy, a major bank restructuring program, and other economic reforms.

Folk dancers in Turkey.

UNITED ARAB EMIRATES

The United Arab Emirates (UAE) is a federation consisting of seven sheikdoms located on the Arabian Gulf. These sheikdoms, also known as emirates, are Abu Dhabi, Dubai, Sharjah, Ras al-Khaimah, Umm al-Qaiwain, Ajman, and al-Fujairah.

Beginning in 1820, Britain entered into treaties with various leaders in the area out of a desire to protect its ships in the Arabian Gulf and the Indian Ocean. In exchange, Britain handled foreign relations for this area, which at this time had been named the Trucial Sates after the truce that the Arab rulers signed with the British in 1853. Relations with Britain continued in this way until 1971, when Britain withdrew from the area, thereby giving the Trucial States their independence. Shortly afterward, the Trucial States merged to form the UAE.

As a federation, the UAE delegates specific powers to the federal government and other powers to the member emirates. Sheikh Zayid bin Sultan al-Nahyan has been the president of the UAE since 1971. This position is elected by the Supreme Council of Rulers, the highest body in the country. There is also a cabinet, and its posts are divided among the emirates. The parliament is known as the Federal National Council (FNC). Its members are appointed by the rulers of each of the emirates to serve two-year terms.

One of the most astonishing things about the UAE is the history of its economy. Since 1962, when petroleum was first exported, the UAE has gone from being an impoverished region of small desert principalities to a modern nation with a standard of living that matches those of most Western European countries.

However, although the UAE's economy is based primarily on oil output, the need to diversify the economy is readily understood. As a result, the government has kept in place the economic reforms implemented during the 1998 oil-price depression. It also has increased spending on job creation and infrastructure expansion, and is opening up utilities to greater private-sector involvement.

YEMEN

Yemen shares a common trait with its Middle Eastern neighbors in that its history stretches back at least 3,000 years. Furthermore, the country saw a succession of rulers before becoming an independent nation: ancient civilizations like the Mineans, the Ethiopians, the Arabs, the Ottomans, and the British. Yemen's independence was finally recognized by Britain in 1925.

However, at that point Yemen was not really a whole, independent nation. Years of civil war between the northern and southern regions of the country led to numerous coups, assassinations, and intense ***guerrilla*** fighting. By the end of 1981, a constitution had been drafted to implement a merger between the two Yemens. However, it was not until 1990 that the merger became official.

Today, Yemen is governed by a republican government with a parliament. The current president is Ali Abdallah Salih. The president is elected by a direct, popular vote for a seven-year term. He appoints the vice president, the prime minister, and the deputy prime ministers. The cabinet, known as the Council of Ministers, is also appointed by the president on the advice of the prime minister.

Yemen is one of the poorest countries in the Arab world. However, with the discovery of some oil in 1972 and the onset of oil production in the mid-1990s, things are starting to change. In addition, there is another potential source of wealth in this country that has yet to be fully explored. Mineral resources, such as zinc, iron, lead, gold, silver, copper, sulfur, and nickel, have not been accurately assessed, but are thought to be large. Yemen has worked hard to maintain a tight control over spending and to implement programs that will modernize and streamline the economy.

An Arab man reads the Qur'an (also spelled Koran), the holy book of Islam. The Qur'an, which was dictated by the Prophet Muhammad, is believed by Muslims to contain the commandments of Allah.

The People

The peoples of the Middle East comprise a diverse group. They have some commonalities, such as locale and religious beliefs, or, in some cases, a shared tribal history. What best characterizes most of the people of the Middle East, however, is the complex role that family and kinship plays in all aspects of life.

There are five primary ethnic or cultural groups in the Middle East. Arabs make up the majority, accounting for almost the entire populations of Egypt, Jordan, Syria, Lebanon, Morocco, Algeria, Tunisia, Libya, the countries of the Arabian Peninsula, and Iraq. The Turks reside primarily in Turkey and Iran. The Persians who are descendants of the pre-Islamic residents of Iran make up about 60 percent of that country's population. Kurds reside in the countries of Turkey, Iran, Iraq, and Syria. The Jewish people are the fifth cultural group in the Middle East. Although Jews come from diverse backgrounds, they share common traditions and heritage.

Due to the growth of the petroleum industry and accompanying modernization, many of the traditional ways of life that dominated the cultures of the Middle East since ancient times have disappeared. There are a few remaining tribes of nomads, but people generally live in either urban communities or rural villages.

Religion is of great importance in the Middle East and is closely linked with both the history and the politics of this region. Three major religions emerged in the Middle East—Judaism, Christianity, and Islam. All of these religions share a monotheistic belief—that there is one supreme god who is creator of the universe. The three religions also share some history and beliefs; however, there are great differences between the practices of these faiths.

After Islam was developed during the seventh century A.D., it spread rapidly throughout the Middle East, eventually moving beyond the region into Africa and Asia. Today, most of the people living in the Middle East are Muslims, those who follow the teachings of the Prophet Muhammad. Jews are concentrated in Israel, with small minorities still living in Iran, Tunisia, Syria, Morocco, Yemen, and Egypt. There are some Christian communities in the Middle East, with the largest ones located in Lebanon, Syria, and Egypt.

A small number of people living in the Middle East, particularly foreign workers who have taken jobs as laborers in the Gulf states, practice Hinduism, Buddhism, or other religions.

KINSHIP AND THE FAMILY

The complex network formed by family relations in the Middle East—particularly in the Arab countries—affects each person's economic, political, and even personal life to an extent that is difficult for Westerners to comprehend. For example, there is a sharp distinction made between maternal and paternal cousins, and an individual's behavior toward them is conducted accordingly. In the Middle East, a person's identity as a member of a family or kin group entitles him or her to certain rights and services, just as it obligates this person to make certain sacrifices on behalf of the kin group.

Middle Eastern kinship systems are extended, patriarchal, hierarchical, patrilineal, and sometimes **endogamous**. The extended family plays a crucial economic, political, and social role in the Middle East. Within the family, authority and respect are given to men and elderly family members of both sexes. Therefore, these individuals have the most power and control in a family.

Men are the primary decision-makers, while women exercise power "behind the scenes." Traditionally, a man's role is to lead, protect, and provide for his family's needs, while a woman's primary role is to make a comfortable home, bear and take care of the children, and basically take care of all the domestic responsibilities that go with keeping a house. However, gender roles in the Middle East are undergoing a change as a result of modernization, urbanization, and Western influence.

It is generally considered preferable for someone to marry within his or her extended family, although the **taboo** against siblings marrying each other is observed. Particularly in the Arab world, marriage is often considered a family and business matter, and many marriages are arranged, often when the prospective bride and groom are quite young. In the past, girls as young as 12 years old could be married, but today, girls are considered to be of marriageable age at about 14 or 15 years old.

WOMEN IN THE MIDDLE EAST

While it is possible to make some generalizations regarding women in the Middle East, it is important to note, as with women all over the world, that regional differences exist regarding women's lives. Class, place of residence, ethnicity, religion, marital status, and age are all factors that affect a Middle Eastern woman's opportunities and experiences in life.

Although there is a wide difference from region to region regarding women's status and political rights, broad reforms regarding education have been widespread. The Arab countries have made some of the greatest gains in the education of women anywhere in the world, more than doubling women's literacy rates in the period from 1970 to 1990. However, to keep this in perspective it is important to note that today, more than half of the adult women in the Arab world are illiterate.

It is more difficult to assess women's economic gains in the Middle East. It is widely acknowledged that national labor force

Women shop at a market in Qatar.

figures do not accurately represent the role women play in Middle Eastern economies. This is due, in large part, to the fact that women's economic activity in the household is largely unmeasured in standard labor-force statistics. In the political world, Middle Eastern women's organized participation can be traced back to the early 20th century, when the push for modernization and social reform and the struggle for independence from colonial domination began.

No woman has ever been the leader of any Middle Eastern country, with the exception of Israel, which had a female prime minister, Golda Meir, and many women cabinet ministers. And, according to studies done by the United Nations, there is less participation by women in Arab political life than in any other region in the world.

Nevertheless, there are six different ways in which women—given the opportunity—participate in politics in the Middle East. They take part in national liberation struggles or revolutionary movements. They serve under "arms" or "branches" of political parties and fronts. They are full-fledged members of political parties and formations. They work in women's organizations or federations created by ruling parties or the government itself. They are members of independent organizations that are not necessarily affiliated with politics. Finally, in certain countries, they can be voters and political candidates themselves. In the political world, things are definitely changing for many women in the Middle East, as they are becoming active in a number of countries.

SOCIAL LIFE AND CELEBRATIONS

In the Arab world, men and women often engage in social affairs separately. In many countries, this separation of the sexes extends to places of prayer, government offices, and even shops. Integration in commercial places, however, does take place in Arab countries like Iraq, Syria, Jordan, and Tunisia.

Most Middle Eastern countries provide free primary and secondary education to all citizens. University education is either free or subsidized by scholarships for those in need. Although in theory primary education is compulsory in all countries, internal conflicts and the great distances between many villages and urban centers often prevent children from attending school. A large portion of school-aged females go through primary and secondary education, but far fewer continue to university level. In more conservative states, such as Saudi Arabia, Qatar, and the UAE, the sexes are educated separately at all levels. Although overall literacy has improved significantly in recent years, it remains low in much of the Middle East when compared to Western figures. Israel has the highest literacy rate in the region, with 95 percent of citizens over age 15 able to read and write. Other countries with higher-than-average literacy rates include Bahrain (88.5 percent),

A technician prepares a document for printing at National Press in Amman, Jordan. Like many countries of the Middle East, in recent years Jordanian businesses have tried to modernize in order to compete in the global economy.

Jordan (86.6 percent), Lebanon (86.4 percent), and Turkey (85 percent).

Islam has had a huge influence on the arts and culture of the Middle East. In accordance with prohibitions in the Qur'an, Muslims do not create representations of people, animals, or objects since it is considered a form of idolatry. As a result, artwork in the Middle East is often composed of intricate and ornate geometrical patterns. Other aspects of arts and culture in the Middle East are particular to the countries from which they hail. Exquisite rugs, fabulous cloaks, intricately designed pottery, great works of fiction, and poetry can be found throughout the Middle East, but none of them is classified as "Middle Eastern."

Population of the Middle East

Algeria
Population: 32,277,942

Ethnic groups: Arab-Berber, 99%; European, 1%

Literacy: 61.6% (male, 73.9%; female, 49%)

Bahrain
Population: 656,397 (includes 228,424 non-nationals)

Ethnic groups: Bahraini Arab, 63%; Asian, 19%; other Arab, 10%; Iranian, 8%

Literacy: 88.5% (male, 91.6%; female, 84.2%) (2002 est.)

Djibouti
Population: 472,810

Ethnic groups: Somali, 60%; Afar, 35%; French, Arab, Ethiopian, Italian, 5%

Literacy: 46.2% (male, 60.3%; female, 32.7%)

Egypt
Population: 70,712,345

Ethnic groups: Eastern Hamitic stock (Egyptians, Bedouins, and Berbers), 99%; Greek, Nubian, Armenian, other European (primarily Italian and French), 1%

Literacy: 51.4% (male, 63.6%; female, 38.8%)

Iran
Population: 66,622,704

Ethnic groups: Persian, 51%; Azeri, 24%; Gilaki and Mazandarani, 8%; Kurd, 7%; Arab, 3%; Lur, 2%; Baloch, 2%; Turkmen, 2%; other, 1%

Literacy: 72.1% (male, 78.4%; female, 65.8%) (1994 est.)

Iraq
Population: 24,001,816

Ethnic groups: Arab, 75%–80%; Kurdish, 15%–20%; Turkoman, Assyrian, other, 5%

Literacy: 58% (male, 70.7%; female, 45%)

Israel
Population: 6,029,529

Ethnic groups: Jewish, 80.1% (Europe/America-born, 32.1%; Israel-born, 20.8%; Africa-born, 14.6%; Asia-born, 12.6%); non-Jewish, 19.9% (mostly Arab)

Literacy: 95% (male, 97%; female, 93%) (1992 est.)

Jordan
Population: 5,307,470

Ethnic groups: Arab, 98%; Circassian, 1%; Armenian 1%

Literacy: 86.6% (male, 93.4%; female, 79.4%)

Kuwait
Population: 2,111,561 (includes 1,159,913 non-nationals)

Ethnic groups: Kuwaiti Arab, 45%; other Arab, 35%; South Asian, 9%; Iranian, 4%; other, 7%

Literacy: 78.6% (male, 82.2%; female, 74.9%)

Lebanon
Population: 3,677,780

Ethnic groups: Arab, 95%; Armenian, 4%; other, 1%

Literacy: 86.4% (male, 90.8%; female, 82.2%) (1997 est.)

Libya
Population: 5,368,585

Ethnic groups: Berber and Arab, 97%; Greeks, Maltese, Italians, Egyptians, Pakistanis, Turks, Indians, Tunisians, other, 3%

Literacy: 76.2% (male, 87.9%; female, 63%)

Mauritania
Population: 2,828,858

Ethnic groups: mixed Maure/black, 40%; Maure, 30%; black, 30%

Literacy: 41.2% (male, 51.5%; female, 31.3%) (2002 est.)

Morocco

Population: 31,167,783

Ethnic groups: Arab-Berber, 99.1%; Jewish, 0.2%; other, 0.7%

Literacy: 43.7% (male, 56.6%; female, 31%)

Oman

Population: 2,713,462 (includes 527,078 non-nationals)

Ethnic groups: Omani Arab, 73%; Pakistani/Baluchi 19%; other 8%

Literacy: approaching 80%

Qatar

Population: 793,341

Ethnic groups: Arab, 40%; Pakistani, 18%; Indian, 18%; Iranian, 10%; other, 14%

Literacy: 79% (male, 79%; female, 80%)

Saudi Arabia

Population: 23,513,330 (includes 5,360,526 non-nationals)

Ethnic groups: Arab, 90%; Afro-Asian, 10%

Literacy: 78% (male, 84.2%; female, 69.5%) (2002 est.)

Somalia

Population: 7,753,310

Ethnic groups: Somali, 85%; Bantu, Arab, other, 15%

Literacy: 37.8% (male, 49.7%; female, 25.8%) (2001 est.)

Sudan

Population: 37,090,298

Ethnic groups: black, 52%; Arab, 39%; Beja, 6%; other, 3%

Literacy: 46.1% (male, 57.7%; female, 34.6%)

Syria

Population: 17,155,814

Ethnic groups: Arab, 90.3%; Kurds, Armenians, and other, 9.7%

Literacy: 70.8% (male, 85.7%; female, 55.8%) (1997 est.)

Tunisia

Population: 9,815,644

Ethnic groups: Arab, 98%; European, 1%; Jewish, other, 1%

Literacy: 66.7% (male: 78.6%; female, 54.6%)

Turkey

Population: 67,308,928

Ethnic groups: Turkish, 80%; Kurdish, 20%

Literacy: 85% (male, 94%; female, 77%) (2000)

United Arab Emirates

Population: 2,445,989 (includes 1,576,472 non-nationals)

Ethnic groups: Emirati Arab, 19%; other Arab or Iranian, 23%; South Asian, 50%; Westerners, East Asians, others, 8%

Literacy: 79.2% (male, 78.9%; female, 79.8%)

Yemen

Population: 18,701,257

Ethnic groups: predominantly Arab; but also Afro-Arab, South Asians, Europeans

Literacy: 38% (male, 53%; female, 26%) (1990 est.)

Population figures are 2002 estimates.

Literacy is the ability of those 15 years of age or older to read and write. Literacy rates are 1995 figures unless otherwise noted.

Source: CIA World Factbook, 2002

A small boat ferries passengers across the Dubai Creek, with the skyline of Dubai in the background. Dubai is one of seven small Arab kingdoms that make up the United Arab Emirates, a federation that was formed in the early 1970s.

Communities

*T*he Middle East is a region with a rich history and diverse peoples. Nowhere is this more evident than in the various communities found throughout the countries of the Middle East. This chapter provides a brief overview of the capitals of the 24 countries of the Middle East, including some history and distinctive features of the cities.

Algiers, a city with a population of over 3 million, is the capital of Algeria. The city itself is divided into two parts. The lower part is the modern city, built by the French, and the upper part is the old city, dominated by the Casbah, a 16th-century fortress built by the Ottomans. Algiers has a major international airport and is the center of a vast network of railways and roads. Its strategic location and harbor have made Algiers a major shipping station and a primary Mediterranean refueling point.

The capital of Bahrain is **Manama**, a city with a population

Algiers, the capital of Algeria, is centrally located on the Mediterranean coast.

of about 150,000. Industries include oil refining, **dhow** building, fishing, and pearling. While the Manama area has been inhabited since at least the 18th century, the city did not become the capital of Bahrain until the 1950s.

The capital of Djibouti, **Djibouti Town**, is an important container-shipment and transshipment point on the shipping lanes of the Red Sea and the Suez Canal. The city's primary sources of revenue are coffee, hides, and salt. In 1995, the population was estimated at 383,000.

Cairo is the capital of Egypt and the largest city in Africa. This site has been inhabited for more than 6,000 years and has served as the capital of many Egyptian civilizations. Its population in 1998 was estimated at 6.8 million. As Egypt's principal commercial, administrative, and tourist center, Cairo contains many cultural institutions, businesses, government offices, universities, and hotels. Local industries include cotton textiles, food products, construction supplies, motor vehicles, aircraft, and chemical fertilizers.

Cairo is also an important center for publishing and other forms of media.

Amman is the capital of Jordan and the country's largest city, with more than 1.2 million inhabitants. It was founded sometime before 3000 B.C. and is the country's major tourist attraction. Originally built on seven hills, it now covers nineteen. A number of industries are located just outside of the city.

Tehran, the capital of Iran and its largest city, has a population of more than 6 million people. Tehran may have been founded as early as the fourth century A.D., and despite invasions by Mongols and Afghans, Tehran had survived. It became the capital of Persia in 1788. Modern industries in Tehran include plants that make automobiles, electrical products, household appliances, plastics, cement, textiles, and processed foods.

The capital of Iraq is **Baghdad** (population 4.4 million), which Arabs call "the City of Peace." The present-day city was established in A.D. 762 and was an important cultural and trade center for centuries. It was the capital city for the Abbasid caliphs until the 13th century, and was also made famous by the story collection *Tales from the Thousand and One Arabian Nights*. Baghdad became capital of the Kingdom of Iraq in 1921. Today, it is Iraq's manufacturing and industrial center, with oil refineries, food-processing plants, tanneries, and textile mills.

Jerusalem is the capital of Israel. Three of the world's major religions—Judaism, Christianity, and Islam—consider Jerusalem to be a sacred city; to Jews, Jerusalem is the holiest city because of its role in their ancient history. Today, Jerusalem includes two distinct sections: East Jerusalem, which has a large Palestinian-Arab population, and West Jerusalem, inhabited almost entirely by Jews. The total population of Jerusalem is about 630,000.

The capital of Kuwait is **Kuwait City** (also known as al-Kuwayt), with an estimated population of nearly 1.1 million people. Kuwait

Throughout history powerful forces have contended for Jerusalem. Since 1967, the city has been controlled by Israel, although Christian and Muslim pilgrims are permitted to visit their holy sites.

City was founded in the 18th century. It is an important port, a hub for petrochemical industries and petroleum shipping, and a trade and financial center.

Beirut is the capital of Lebanon, with a population estimated at between 3 and 4 million. (No official census has been taken since 1932.) This is Lebanon's largest city, and was an international banking and cultural center prior to the 1971–91 civil war. Silk and cotton fabrics, as well as gold and silver objects, are the primary manufactures in Beirut today.

The capital of Libya is **Tripoli**, with an estimated population of more than 1 million people. This is the largest city in Libya, as well as the country's principal seaport and leading commercial and manufacturing sector. Major manufactures include processed food, textiles, clothing, construction materials, and tobacco products.

The capital of Mauritania is **Nouakchott**. It has a population of about 600,000, and is the country's primary administrative and economic center. Nouakchott was selected to be the capital in 1957.

The capital of Morocco is **Rabat**. Its population is estimated at more than 1.4 million people. Rabat was originally established in the 12th century as a military post; it became the capital of French Morocco in 1912, and remained the capital when the country gained independence in 1956. Today, as one of Morocco's main ports, it sees considerable shipping activity. Major industries in Rabat include the manufacture of textiles, processed food, and building materials. Government activities, tourism, and handicraft production are also important to the city's economy.

Muscat is the capital of Oman and is the country's largest city. It is Oman's chief administrative center and remains an important port. Muscat became the capital of Oman in 1970. The population of Muscat is 635,000.

Doha is the capital of Qatar and its largest city (population 392,384). It has a large, artificial deepwater port, which serves as a major transshipment center for the cargo of the Arabian Gulf nations. In addition to petroleum, shrimping and shrimp process-ing are important industries in Doha.

In 1824, **Riyadh** was made the seat of the Al Saud family, and it became the capital of Saudi Arabia in 1932. Its population is about 4.3 million. Riyadh is the commercial, educational, and administrative center of Saudi Arabia, and is served by an interna-tional airport and an extensive network of roads and railways. Manufactures include construction materials, refined petroleum, and processed foods.

The capital of Somalia is **Mogadishu**, with an estimated population of about a million people. Mogadishu was founded in the early 10th century by Arab merchants; today it is Somalia's largest city and primary seaport. It is also the country's leading commercial and manufacturing sector, although economic activities were seriously disrupted by civil war. Principal manufactures include processed foods (particularly meat and fish), leather, wood products, and textiles.

The capital of Sudan is **Khartoum**. The city was founded in 1821 as an Egyptian military outpost for captured territory in Sudan. By the 1880s, it was a flourishing commercial and trade center. It was the capital of Anglo-Egyptian Sudan from 1899 to 1955, and became the capital of independent Sudan in 1956. With an estimated population of 924,505, Khartoum is the economic center of Sudan and its largest urban area. Manufacturing industries include printing, food processing, and textile and glass manufacturing.

The capital of Syria is **Damascus**, with an estimated population of 1.9 million. Damascus is said to be the world's oldest inhabited city. It has been a major city in the Aramean Kingdom, the Greek Empire, the Roman Empire, and the Ottoman Empire. In ancient times, Damascus was noted for its dried fruit, wine, wool, linens, silk, and steel sword blades. Industries in Damascus today include the weaving of silk cloth and the making of leather goods; filigreed gold and silver objects; and inlaid wooden, copper, and brass items. Other manufactures are food, clothing, and printed material.

The capital of Tunisia is **Tunis**, with a population of 674,000. Scholars believe that Tunis was founded by the Phoenicians in the sixth century B.C. The Romans, the Arabs, and the French all had control over it, and the French built the modern city during their rule (1881–1956). Today, Tunis is a significant commercial and industrial center, with plants producing chemicals, processed foods, and textiles.

Ankara (population 3 million) is the capital of Turkey. Ankara has been a trading center since ancient times. The Hittites, the

The Galata Tower rises above buildings in Istanbul, Turkey. The historic ruins and beautiful scenery of Turkey make the country attractive to tourists.

Greeks, the Romans, the Byzantines, the Arabs, and the Turks all had control over this city at one time or another. In the 13th century the name was changed to Angora. In 1923, after the establishment of the Republic of Turkey, the capital was moved from Istanbul to Angora. The name was changed back to Ankara in 1930.

The capital of the UAE is the city of **Abu Dhabi** (population 605,000), which is located in the emirate of the same name. It is a financial, transportation, and communications center for a region that is rich in petroleum, and is also home to an international airport and an artificial deepwater harbor. In addition to petroleum, other products include steel pipe and cement.

The capital of Yemen is **Sanaa**, the commercial center for a huge fruit-growing region. The eastern section of Sanaa, known as the old city, is famous for its jewelry, silver and leather goods, silks, and carpets. Sanaa's population is about 1 million. Another city in Yemen, Aden, is one of the busiest ports in the world.

FLAGS OF THE MIDDLE EAST

ALGERIA

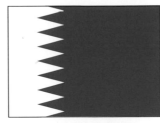

BAHRAIN

DJIBOUTI

EGYPT

IRAN

IRAQ

ISRAEL

JORDAN

KUWAIT

LEBANON

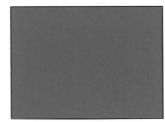

LIBYA

MAURITANIA

MOROCCO

OMAN

QATAR

FLAGS OF THE MIDDLE EAST

SAUDI ARABIA

SOMALIA

SUDAN

SYRIA

TUNISIA

TURKEY

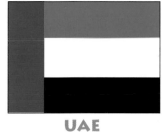

UAE

YEMEN

9000 B.C.: The earliest farming communities are established in Mesopotamia.

6000 B.C.: Elamites begin building civilizations in Persia (modern-day Iran).

3500 B.C.: Sumerian civilization is established in Mesopotamia, with major cities at Ur and Kish.

ca. 3100 B.C.: Lower and Upper Egypt are united into a single kingdom with its capital at Memphis.

ca. 2700–2200 B.C.: The era of the Old Kingdom of ancient Egypt; Egypt's rulers build the great pyramids.

ca. 1750 B.C.: The Sumerian ruler Hammurabi establishes his code of laws.

332 B.C.: Alexander the Great of Macedon conquers Egypt; Hellenistic culture and values begin to spread throughout the Middle East.

146 B.C.: Roman forces end the Third Punic War with the destruction of Carthage; Rome soon after becomes the most important power in the Middle East.

A.D. 330: Constantinople, in modern-day Turkey, becomes the center of the Eastern Roman Empire (or Byzantine Empire).

632: The Prophet Muhammad dies, but the religion that he preached, Islam, continues to spread throughout the region.

1453: Constantinople falls to the Ottoman Turks, who soon spread their empire throughout the Middle East.

1869: The Suez Canal is completed.

1919: The end of World War I leads to the formation of the League of Nations; the Ottoman Empire is broken into smaller states, each of which are placed under the control of France or Great Britain.

1962: After a bloody eight-year civil war, Algeria gains its independence from France.

1971: The Arab states of the Gulf gain independence from Great Britain.

1978: At a meeting at the U.S. presidential retreat at Camp David, Maryland, Egyptian president Anwar Sadat and Israeli prime minister Menachem Begin agree to a peace treaty that comes to be known as the Camp David Accords.

1979: The people of Iran, led by the Ayatollah Khomeini, overthrow the government of the shah and install a theocracy.

CHRONOLOGY

1981: The Gulf Cooperation Council, an organization of Arab Gulf states, is formed for mutual defense and shared economic projects.

1988: The eight-year-long Iran-Iraq War ends.

1990: The Taif Accord ends the Lebanese civil war; in August, Iraq invades Kuwait.

1991: The United States leads an international coalition to drive Iraqi forces out of Kuwait.

2000: The Israeli-Palestinian peace process breaks down, and a violent *intifada* begins.

2001: Al-Qaeda terrorists strike the United States on September 11.

2002: Increased violence between Palestinians and Israelis threatens to destabilize Middle East; U.N. weapons inspectors return to Iraq.

2003: The United States, convinced that the regime of Iraqi president Saddam Hussein is carrying weapons of mass destruction, leads an invasion that topples Saddam's regime; an interim government is installed.

agrarian—characteristic of farmers or their way of life.

anarchy—the state of disorder due to an absence of government.

aquifer—a water-bearing stratum of permeable rock, sand, or gravel.

arable—fit for or used for the growing of crops.

aridity—the measure of how dry and how poor a region is for agriculture.

armistice—a suspension of fighting by an agreement between two opponents.

artisan—a person who is skilled in a trade or craft.

autonomy—the state of self-governance.

Bedouin—a nomadic Arab of the Arabian, Syrian, or North African deserts.

cirque—a deep steep-walled basin on a mountain that usually forms the end of a valley.

coup—a brilliant and sudden overthrow of a government and seizure of political power.

dhow—an Arab boat rigged with triangular sails.

endogamous—pertaining to marriage within a specific group as required by custom or law.

extradite—to return an alleged criminal to an authority having jurisdiction over him or her.

gross domestic product—the total value of goods and services produced within a country in a one-year period.

guerrilla—a person who engages in irregular warfare and is a member of an independent unit that usually has a particular political objective.

industrialization—the act of engaging in industry.

inflation—an increase in the volume of money and credit relative to available goods and services resulting in higher prices.

isthmus—a narrow strip of land connecting two larger land areas.

junta—a group of persons controlling a government, usually after a revolutionary seizure of power.

pastoral—of or relating to the countryside.

populism—a political philosophy that aims to represent the common people.

salinization—the introduction of salt to soil.

GLOSSARY

sanction—an economic or military coercive measure usually adopted by a group of nations in order to force a nation violating international law to desist or yield to prosecution.

socialist—relating to economic and political theories advocating collective or governmental ownership and administration of the means of production and distribution of goods.

sovereignty—freedom from outside interference and the right to self-government.

steppe—one of the vast treeless and semiarid tracts in southeastern Europe or Asia.

subversive—someone who attempts to overthrow or undermine a government or political system by working secretly from within.

taboo—a prohibition imposed by social custom or as a protective measure.

textile—a woven or knit cloth.

theocratic—relating to government of a state by immediate divine guidance or by priestly figures.

unicameral—consisting of a single legislative chamber.

FURTHER READING

Bowen, Donna Lee, and Evelyn A. Early. *Everyday Life in the Muslim Middle East.* 2nd ed. Bloomington: Indiana University Press, 2002.

Crystal, Jill. *Oil and Politics in the Gulf.* Cambridge, England: Cambridge University Press, 1994.

Gerner, Deborah J., editor. *Understanding the Contemporary Middle East.* Boulder, Colo.: Lynne Rienner Publishers, 2000.

Hourani, Albert. *A History of the Arab Peoples.* Cambridge, Mass.: Belknap Press of the University of Harvard Press, 1991.

Kechichian, Joseph A., ed., *Iran, Iraq, and the Arab Gulf States.* New York: Palgrave, 2001.

Laqueur, Walter, and Barry Rubin. *The Arab-Israeli Reader.* New York: Penguin, 2001

Lesche, David W. *1979: The Year that Shaped the Modern Middle East.* Boulder, Colo.: Westview Press, 2001.

Lewis, Bernard. *Islam in History: Ideas, People, and Events in the Middle East.* Chicago: Open Court Publishing, 1993.

————. *The Middle East: A Brief History of the Last 2,000 Years.* New York: Scribner, 1995.

Ryan, Stephen. *The United Nations and International Politics.* New York: St. Martin's Press, 2000.

Shakir, M. H., trans. *The Qur'an.* Elmhurst, N.Y.: Tahrike Tarsile Quran, Inc., 1995.

Surrat, Robin, ed. *The Middle East, 9th ed.* Washington, D.C.: Congressional Quarterly Press, 2000.

Viorst, Milton. *Sandcastles: The Arabs in Search of the Modern World.* New York: Alfred Knopf, 1994.

Williams, Mary E., editor. *The Middle East: Opposing Viewpoints.* San Diego, Calif.: Greenhaven Press, 2000.

Zahlan, Rosemarie Said. *The Making of the Modern Gulf States: Kuwait, Bahrain, Qatar, the United Arab Emirates, and Oman.* Reading, England: Garnet Publishing, Ltd., 1999.

INTERNET RESOURCES

http://www.arab.net/index.html

This site provides general information about the countries of the Middle East as well as links to current events.

http://www.odci.gov/cia/publications/factbook/

The CIA World Factbook is a great resource for anyone needing basic facts and figures on the countries of the Middle East.

http://www.albany.edu/history/middle-east/

This website provides information and links on the history, cultures, and societies of the Middle East.

http://www.metimes.com/2K2/issue2002-39/front_index.htm

An extensive website that provides in-depth news articles about events, people, and places in the Middle East.

http://www.albawaba.com/main/index.ie.php3?lang=e

News articles, country information, web links, and more are found on the the Middle East Gateway site.

http://www.mideastinfo.com/

The Middle East Information Network site provides information on education, religion, news, business, travel, and more.

Numbers in **bold italic** refer to captions.

INDEX

history, 18–19
    Arab-Israeli conflict, 20, 46–48, 51–53,
       63–64
    Arab Revolt, 42–43
    Crusades, 35
    independence and nationalism, 18, 39–45
    Iran-Iraq War, 50, 61, 62
    Islamic Revolution (1979), 20, 48–51
    Mamluks, 35
    Mongols, 35
    Ottoman Empire, 25, 35–38, 39–40, 42, 78
    Persian Gulf War, *33*
    Roman Empire, 33–34
    Seljuk Turks, 34–35
Hussein, Saddam, 50, 51, 53, 62–63, 67
    See also Iraq
Hussein, Sharif, 65
Hussein (King), 65–66

independence. *See* history
industry, 38, 44
intifada, 48, 53
    See also Arab-Israeli conflict; Palestine
       Liberation Organization (PLO)
Iran, 23, *28*, 45, 48–51, 54–55, 61–62, *90*
Iranian Revolution. *See* Islamic Revolution
    (1979)
Iraq, *28–29*, *33*, 43–44, 45, 46, 53, 62–63, 87, *90*
    and 2003 war against, 53, 62, 63
    and the Iran-Iraq War, 50, 61
    and the Persian Gulf War, 51, 67
Islam, *15*, 19–20, *37*, 50, 53, *57*, 67–68, 77, 84,
    89, 95
    See also Christianity; Judaism
Islamic Revolution (1979), 20, 48–51, 62
    See also Iran
Israel, 18, *29*, 45–48, 51, 55, 63–65, 84, 87, *90*
    See also Arab-Israeli conflict

Jerusalem, *15*, 35, 46, 63–64, 95, *96*
Jordan, 18, *29*, 43–44, 45, 46, 48, 51, 63, 65–66,
    87, *90*
Jordan River, 27
Judaism, *15*, 19, 20, 77, 84, 95

    See also Christianity; Islam; Israel

Khamanei, Ayatollah Seyyed Ali, 55
Khartoum, Sudan, 98
Khatemi, Mohammed, 54–55
Khomeini, Ayatollah, *49*, 50
    See also Islamic Revolution (1979)
Koran. *See* Qur'an
Koutoubia Mosque, *57*
Ksar Ouled, *76*
Kublai Khan, 35
Kuwait, *29*, *33*, 45, 50, 51, 66–67, *90*
Kuwait City, Kuwait, *65*, 95–96
al-Kuwayt. *See* Kuwait City, Kuwait

Lahoud, Emile, 67
League of Nations, *41*, 43
    See also United Nations
Lebanon, *29*, *34*, 43–44, 45, 46, 51, 63, 67–69,
    90
Libya, *29*, 69–70, *90*
literacy rate, 86, 88–89, *90–91*
    See also education
Lloyd George, David, *41*

Maghreb, 16
    See also Middle East
Mamluks, 35
    See also history
Manama, Bahrain, 93–94
mandates, ruling, *41*, 43–44, 65
    See also history
maps, 12–13, *38*
Mashrakh, 16
    See also Middle East
Mauritania, 16, *29*, 70, *90*
Mecca, 73, *74*
Medina, 73, *74*
Meir, Golda, 87
Middle East
    area, 15, 24–25, 26
    climate, 18, 25, 26, *28–31*
    countries of the, 15–18, 25, *28–31*
    economy, 44–45, 53, 59–60, 62, 65, 72–73,

INDEX/PICTURE CREDITS

CONTRIBUTORS

The FOREIGN POLICY RESEARCH INSTITUTE (FPRI) served as editorial consultants for the MODERN MIDDLE EAST NATIONS series. FPRI is one of the nation's oldest "think tanks." The Institute's Middle East Program focuses on Gulf security, monitors the Arab-Israeli peace process, and sponsors an annual conference for teachers on the Middle East, plus periodic briefings on key developments in the region.

Among the FPRI's trustees is a former Secretary of State and a former Secretary of the Navy (and among the FPRI's former trustees and interns, two current Undersecretaries of Defense), not to mention two university presidents emeritus, a foundation president, and several active or retired corporate CEOs.

The scholars of FPRI include a former aide to three U.S. Secretaries of State, a Pulitzer Prize–winning historian, a former president of Swarthmore College and a Bancroft Prize–winning historian, and two former staff members of the National Security Council. And the FPRI counts among its extended network of scholars—especially its Inter-University Study Groups—representatives of diverse disciplines, including political science, history, economics, law, management, religion, sociology, and psychology.

DR. HARVEY SICHERMAN is president and director of the Foreign Policy Research Institute in Philadelphia, Pennsylvania. He has extensive experience in writing, research, and analysis of U.S. foreign and national security policy, both in government and out. He served as Special Assistant to Secretary of State Alexander M. Haig Jr. and as a member of the Policy Planning Staff of Secretary of State James A. Baker III. Dr. Sicherman was also a consultant to Secretary of the Navy John F. Lehman Jr. (1982–1987) and Secretary of State George Shultz (1988).

A graduate of the University of Scranton (B.S., History, 1966), Dr. Sicherman earned his Ph.D. at the University of Pennsylvania (Political Science, 1971), where he received a Salvatori Fellowship. He is author or editor of numerous books and articles, including *America the Vulnerable: Our Military Problems and How to Fix Them* (FPRI, 2002) and *Palestinian Autonomy, Self-Government and Peace* (Westview Press, 1993). He edits *Peacefacts*, an FPRI bulletin that monitors the Arab-Israeli peace process.

LISA MCCOY is a freelance writer and editor living in Washington State. Her books in the MODERN MIDDLE EAST series include *United Arab Emirates*, *Qatar*, and *Bahrain*. She is currently at work on a novel.